Chocolate
for Breakfast

Chocolate for Breakfast

Entertaining Menus to Start the Day with a Celebration

FROM NAPA VALLEY'S OAK KNOLL INN

BARBARA PASSINO

PHOTOGRAPHY BY **MARC HOBERMAN**

THE GERALD & MARC HOBERMAN COLLECTION

CAPE TOWN · LONDON · NEW YORK

Photography and color reproduction: Marc Hoberman
Production control: Gerald Hoberman
Layout and design: Mellany Fick, Gerald Hoberman, Marc Hoberman, Melanie Kriel
Text: Barbara Passino
Recipe collaborator: Shirlee Quick
Editor: Laurie Rose-Innes
Specialist editorial consultant: Antonia Allegra
Indexer: Joy Clack

www.hobermancollection.com

For more information about Oak Knoll Inn, please visit www.oakknollinn.com

ISBN: 978-1-919939-55-1   ISBN: 1-919939-55-5

Chocolate for Breakfast is published by The Gerald & Marc Hoberman Collection (Pty) Ltd
Reg. No. 99/00167/07. PO Box 60044, Victoria Junction, 8005, Cape Town, South Africa
Telephone: 27-21-419 6657/419 2210 Fax: 27-21-425 4410 e-mail: office@hobermancollection.com

International marketing and corporate sales

United States of America, Canada, Asia
Hoberman Collection (USA), Inc. / Una Press, Inc.
PO Box 880206, Boca Raton, FL 33488, USA
Telephone: (561) 542 1141
e-mail: hobcolus@bellsouth.net

United Kingdom, Republic of Ireland, Europe
Hoberman Collection (UK)
250 Kings Road, London, SW3 5UE
Telephone: 0207 352 1315 Fax: 0207 681 0064
e-mail: uksales@hobermancollection.com

Agents and distributors

United States of America, Canada
Perseus Distribution
387 Park Avenue South
New York NY 10016
Tel: (212) 340 8100 / Fax: (212) 340 8195

London
DJ Segrue Ltd
7c Bourne Road, Bushey, Hertfordshire WD23 3NH
Tel: (0)7976 273 225 / Fax: (0)20 8421 9577
e-mail: sales@djsegrue.co.uk

South Africa
Hoberman Collection
6 Victoria Junction, Prestwich Street, Green Point
Tel: +27 (0)21 419 6657 / Fax: +27 (0)21 425 4410
e-mail: office@hobermancollection.com

United Kingdom, Europe and Far East
John Rule Sales & Marketing
40 Voltaire Road, London SW4 6DH
Tel: 020 7498 0115
email: johnrule@johnrule.co.uk

Printed in Singapore

To Dad, for the chocolate-loving DNA,

Mom, who made chocolate my first solid food,

and Aunt Johnny, who taught me it was for breakfast

Oak Knoll Inn, Napa Valley

Contents

Acknowledgements

We may have grown up in different hemispheres, but I know **Marc Hoberman** and I are genetically linked by a common passion for chocolate. He spent four weeks with us photographing dishes for the cookbook, coaching me, and creating much more of this book than the luscious photos. Now a member of the Oak Knoll family, Marc wins the prize for strangest eating habits of all of the guests we've had in sixteen years – and there's some stiff competition for that title. He eats nothing "luscious and juicy" (like fruit) no eggs, sauces… but as he was apparently a dragon in another life, he'll eat anything Chinese – or at least that's his explanation. A lifelong chocoholic, as long as we kept him in his drug of choice, he produced magnificent food photography. His clever wit, treasure trove of stories and unique take on the world kept us laughing and in high spirits through a rigorous shooting schedule. Marc, I can't wait to start the next book. Well, maybe a week or two.

And I must thank Marc's father, the very talented **Gerald Hoberman**, who was the first to have faith and say he'd love to publish my cookbook. We met while they were here creating their glorious Napa book. Ever the grateful soul, I complained and asked them to come back to take another shot, and we still became friends, linked by a common aesthetic and sense of whimsy.

Shirlee Quick is my kitchen soul-mate and co-conspirator. Responsible for preparing and creating a number of these recipes, she's the one I consult when the quince tree is loaded or the tyranny of the tomatoes has begun. A talented and experienced restaurant chef with a marvelous palate, she devises detailed itineraries to introduce our guests to the joys of Napa's food and wine, arranging visits to small specialized wineries, olive oil producers, food purveyors, and Napa's fine restaurants.

In this, she's ably aided by **Vikki Rugg**. Vikki's family were founders of Napa and if you want to know why those cows on the Silverado Trail look so raggedy, or the cemetery is where it is, she'll have the answer. A delight to work with, Vikki joined us after a try-out at our evening wine party (she passed with high marks) and on the proviso that she could not cook. That didn't last long. She's now the breakfast chef two days a week – a testament to the ease of preparing and joy of serving some of these menus.

Maria Hernandez has helped me in the kitchen for so long that we barely need to speak. I turn around to get a cookie sheet, and she's already prepped it for baking and turned on the oven. I decide to make squash flowers and notice she's coming in from the garden with a basket full. She knows every edible flower and herb in our garden and arranges them like the professional she is.

Tony Kruglinski has been a friend longer than I've known my husband. When I walk out of the kitchen to greet guests at breakfast and all heads turn to look at me, I know he's been telling them something interesting – like "Don't you think she's doing well now that she's out on parole?" When I said *Chocolate for Breakfast* was finally in the works, he created poems for me on the topic (pages 109 & 219).

10

To the many guests who've encouraged me to write this cookbook, tested the recipes and given me feedback – thank you. **Gary** and **Treasure Wheeler**, **Alex Duda** and **John Rieber**, **Herb** and **Lanatter Fox**, **Patty** and **Lloyd Kendall**, **Karen** and **Bruce Evans**, **Mark** and **Kate Rowe**, **Diana** and **Bob Odermatt**, **Diane** and **Paul Thompson**, **Joe** and **Jean Stothert** – I know I'm going to be in trouble because the list is so long and I've only noted a few of you who've been here twenty times or more – thank you for the love and support.

David Jackson and **Craig Claussen**, former owners of La Residence, are responsible for our finding Oak Knoll Inn and for teaching us how to be Innkeepers. They were the ones we turned to with "and what do we do when they do THAT?" and always got a funny and sensible answer. They bailed me out when the propane company failed or the lights went out, and were always there to help fix those things that go wrong in the night.

As this book neared reality, **Toni Allegra** and **Joanne Weir** not only encouraged me but provided invaluable suggestions, resources and insights into the mysterious world of cookbook publishing. Toni raced back from Mexico to give one last round of thoughtful editing. You made this first timer feel like a pro.

And of course, **John**, my husband of thirty years, whom I fire about once a week, is the one who makes it possible for me to still be doing this after sixteen years. Although I said I'd marry him for better or worse, but not for 24 hours a day, he's the one who gets up at 4:00 in the morning to make coffee for guests with an early flight, picks up the phone when I'm covered with flour, runs to the store, pours a mean glass of CHAMPAGNE and generally makes it all much more fun and definitely much sillier. Thank you Beepers.

Attribution

Paula Wolfert, cookbook hall of fame author, maintains that she's never created a recipe, she's just researched and written them. I've never been quite sure when to give someone else credit for a recipe that was a starting point for one of mine, and when that would be more insulting than gratifying.

I remember asking my mother one day what she was making. "Betty Van Etten's chicken tetrazzini," she said.

"Really? I'm surprised. I've had Mrs Van Etten's dish and it's delicious, but Dad doesn't eat Parmesan cheese and he doesn't like mushrooms. And isn't that turkey you're cutting up?"

"Well," she explained, "I leave out the mushrooms and substitute aged cheddar for the Parmesan. We had the turkey left from that breast I cooked the other night. And I've found that if I use cream of chicken soup I don't have to make that sauce."

At that point my Dad walked into the kitchen and asked "What are you making for dinner?"

"Betty Van Etten's chicken tetrazinni," said Mom.

So to all of you who feel I've filched parts of your recipe, I apologize. And for those of you who feel I haven't been true to yours but gave you credit for it – I apologize for that, too.

Introduction

"Almost every person has something secret he likes to eat."
M.F.K. FISHER

There's something deliciously naughty about eating dessert first. As the world's favorite flavor, chocolate is hardly a secret indulgence. Eating it for breakfast often is, but I've vowed to share this treat with others, offering chocolate as an appetizer, main course, or as a grace note in a well-rounded menu designed to encourage our upstanding guests to sit down and finish their breakfast.

With dishes as heart-healthy as a crisp dark chocolate tortilla brimming with fresh fruit and berries, or as decadent as chocolate toast pillows that ooze melted chocolate when your fork breaks through the beignet-like crust, this book is for those who want to start the day with a celebration, whether entertaining friends on the weekend or creating a romantic breakfast for two.

The eggs, bacon and pancakes send-them-back-out-to-the-plow menu of our American farming heritage would send most of us back to bed. In the evolution of American cuisine, breakfast has stayed under the covers.

When we came to the Inn in 1992, I took a look at breakfast through a winking eye and did what any warm-blooded American does with tradition – tampered with it. Taking Latin American, Mediterranean and Asian influences, combined with the fresh local ingredients that have come to define California cuisine, we created menus that start the morning by alerting your sensual arsenal that this will be no ordinary day.

Barbara Passino

Chocolate – a delicious history *

BY MARC HOBERMAN

* may contain nuts

A guilty indulgence, a food of celebration, an end-goal for pocket money, an aphrodisiac (Casanova swore by his daily "fix"), a reason to start the diet "next Monday" and a likely ending to "Love is…" Chocolate is many things to many people.

From the altars of the ancient Aztecs to the breakfast table at Oak Knoll Inn, the illustrious history of chocolate is fascinating and often surprising.

At some point in all our lives we have discovered chocolate; mine came from that guilty overloaded finger of chocolate batter while my mother baked a chocolate cake on a summer's morning. Barbara's first solid food in life was a chocolate brownie used as a bribe by a breast-feeding mother at an inconvenient time. Reportedly, it was the occasion of her first smile. During the making of this book, we both smiled a lot.

But who discovered it first? Contrary to the commonly held belief that it was an older sibling who got there before you, chocolate is believed to have been discovered by the ancient Maya in the tropical rainforest of the Americas. It quickly gained popularity amongst the ancient cultures of Mexico and Central America and was adopted by the Aztec empire that dominated much of Mesoamerica by 1400 A.D. Keeping in mind that this was long before Milton Hershey was around, the Aztecs decided that this curious bean tasted like "bitter water" and gave it that name in their Aztec tongue – *xocolatl* or *chocolatl*.

As *xocolatl* tends to do when introduced to civilizations, it rapidly became integral in everyday Aztec life. Cacao seeds *(Theobroma cacao)* became a convenient currency of the time, a tax for citizens and an instrument of tribute paid by the conquered. The gods got involved as well. According to Aztec belief, cacao was brought to earth by the god Quetzalcoatl who was consequently banished from paradise for this blasphemous act of giving to humankind the sacred drink which the gods deemed to be their own celestial preserve. In response, the Aztec made chocolate offerings to their gods, and the Maya paid homage to their own special god of cacao growers and merchants, Ek Chuah. Funny to think that so many years later when mortal men are banished from Paradise by their female counterparts they often return with chocolate offerings. But more of that later.

With the conquest of Mexico in 1521, the Spanish conquistadors had their first encounter with chocolate and soon discovered its delicious flavor, nutritional content and restorative effect. With Montezuma's warriors defeated, conquistadors demanded the Aztec nobles' much-loved cacao as spoils of war. The Spanish began to add sugar (not known to the Mesoamericans) as well as cinnamon and other spices to the chocolate mix.

Today's modern technology makes hiding even one chocolate bar quite difficult, but when chocolate first arrived in Spain it remained a secret for almost 100 years before reaching the rest of Europe. When it did finally reach the whole of Europe, it became an elite beverage among the upper classes and a status symbol.

Chocolate's popularity began to spread like…melted chocolate. In the 18th century, chocolate was the cardinals' drink of choice and is believed to have been served even while electing a new Pope. In Mexico during *Dia de los Muertos* (Day of the Dead), cacao seeds and hot chocolate are offered on altars to welcome the departed souls of loved ones.

But little Johnny was not about to get his hands on a chocolate bar just yet. In France, chocolate became a state monopoly and only the aristocrats were permitted to drink it. The self-confessed chocoholic queen, Anne of Austria (daughter of King Philip III of Spain) who married Louis XIII of France in 1615, ensured its popularity.

England stepped in with a great invention that helped get chocolate closer to our plate. During the late 1600s, Sir Hans Sloane, President of the Royal College of Physicians, had the great idea of mixing cocoa with milk, resulting in a smoother texture and lighter consistency that the "masses" could enjoy without the need for much of an "acquired taste." But now they could actually acquire the taste – London's first chocolate house (the forerunner of coffee shops) opened for business in 1657. They were rather agreeable places of social discourse, politics, gaming, business and the like.

As demand for chocolate grew, the English turned to their favourite pastime and colonized suitable cacao-growing farm lands in Ceylon (Sri Lanka), the Dutch established plantations in Java, Sumatra and Venezuela and the French grew cacao in the West Indies.

Enter a fantastic Frenchman named Doret in the early 1700s, who developed a machine for grinding cacao seeds into a paste. He was followed by another Frenchman (also fantastic), Dubuisson, who produced a steam-driven chocolate mill. Chocolate could now be mass-produced relatively inexpensively. This, as well as new chocolate recipes and manufacturing techniques, facilitated the transformation of hot chocolate's relatively oily, somewhat gritty paste dissolved with water or milk into a sweet, smooth, creamy, delicious, solid chocolate bar.

The first chocolate factory in colonial America was established in 1765. By 1828 Coenraad Van Houten, a Dutch chemist, had invented the cacao press, separating cacao butter from cacao powder and enabling consistent and cheaper chocolate manufacture.

In 1815 Van Houten added alkaline salts to the cacao powder, making it more water-soluble, as well as imparting a milder flavor and richer color; and in 1875, Henri Nestlé and Daniel Peter teamed up to produce "milk chocolate" by adding condensed milk to the mix. This silky, creamy, sweet brown chocolate soon became universally loved. Little Johnny could now at last have his chocolate bar.

Soon after, Hershey produced chocolate-coated caramels, and the father and son team of Mars produced malted-milk fillings. Many creative chocolatiers were to produce an infinite variety of chocolate treats.

In 1824 a young Quaker named John Cadbury opened a one-man business in Bull Street, Birmingham. This was to be the foundation of Cadbury Limited, now one of the world's largest producers of chocolate. His first advertisement in the *Birmingham Gazette* on 1 March 1824 was succinct and had a great last three words that seemed to have been lost on the world until quite recently: *John Cadbury is desirous of introducing to particular notice "Cocoa Nibs," prepared by himself, an article affording a most nutritious beverage for breakfast.*

Fast forward a few decades and we are seated in the leafy gardens of Oak Knoll Inn, situated in the middle of 600 acres of Napa Valley vines. A table of guests from around the world chat and laugh as they wait in anticipation of sampling one of Barbara's famous breakfasts with a chocolate twist. As with all good things in life, chocolate can be discovered again and again. Guests often book an extra night.

Nine out of ten scientists agree that after reading this you will feel like indulging in a nice piece of creamy chocolate. Go on, don't feel bad, get yourself a bar or a block or a slice and turn the page to discover a new world of chocolate – the spectacular breakfasts with a chocolate twist at the Oak Knoll Inn.

Marc Hoberman
CHOCOLATE MILKSHAKE CONNOISSEUR

Ingredient Standards

Large eggs

All purpose flour, scooped and measured, not sifted first unless specified

Butter, sweet (unsalted)

cream = heavy cream, not ultra-pasteurized (under "Ingredients" on the label, it should just say "cream")

Whole or 2% milk

Kosher, sea, grey or other good quality salt

Nutmeg, freshly grated

Pepper, black, freshly grated, Tellicherry recommended

Pure vanilla extract

Cocoa powder = good quality cocoa powder, either "dutched" or "alkalized" or natural

Do not use mixtures intended for hot chocolate (e.g. Nestlé's Quick)

Chocolate in many forms

Solid chocolate

There is no difference between cooking and eating chocolate, although occasionally "cooking chocolate" on a label refers to unsweetened chocolate. If it tastes good, it's eating chocolate. If it doesn't, why cook with it?

Frequently quality chocolatiers will list a percentage on the label. This indicates by weight the amount of ingredients derived from the cacao bean. The remaining percentage is sugar and sometimes a small amount of vanilla or other spice and perhaps soy lecithin as a stabilizer. For example, Scharffen Berger's 70% bittersweet has more cacao and less sugar than their 62% semi-sweet chocolate. A 99% cacao includes no sugar at all.

Cocoa Powder

Cocoa powder is made by pressing some of the cocoa butter out of roasted cacao beans. This is "natural" cocoa powder.

The powder can then be "dutched" or "alkalized", a process of washing the cocoa with an alkaline substance such as potassium carbonate to reduce harshness and acidity. This process makes for a more consistent product with a predictable pH. Packaging should indicate whether the cocoa has been dutched. These cocoas tend to be very dark, like Valrhona. Natural cocoas, like that made by Scharffen Berger, are much lighter in color.

Except in baking, they can be used interchangeably. Natural cocoa can throw off the effects of baking powder or baking soda. All of the recipes in this book have been tested and can be made with either type of cocoa powder.

Chocolate nibs

Chocolate or cacao nibs taste like chocolaty unsweetened nuts. They are the roasted and chopped nut of the cacao bean with the outer hull removed. Substitute them for walnuts or peanuts in baking recipes or on top of a baby banana split, and you won't have to worry about people with nut allergies.

White "chocolate"

It's not really chocolate if it's white. Once cacao beans are pressed to make cocoa powder, the remaining fat is cocoa butter. That fat is combined with sugar, vanilla and milk to make white "chocolate". It picks up flavor from the cocoa butter, but is not the real thing. Use white chocolate for those times when lack of color matters more than depth of flavor.

Metric measurements

US measurements converted to metric
Rounding has been used

Volume and liquid measures

½ teaspoon	2 ml	
1 teaspoon	5 ml	
1 tablespoon	15 ml	
¼ cup	60 ml	
⅓ cup	80 ml	
½ cup	125 ml	
⅔ cup	150 ml	
¾ cup	200 ml	
1 cup	250 ml	
4 cups	1 liter	
1 pint	2 cups	500 ml

Weights

1 ounce	30 grams
3 ounces	90 grams
4 ounces (¼ pound)	115 grams
1 pound (16 ounces)	450 grams

Length

1 inch	25 mm
6 inch	152 mm
10 inch	254 mm

Oven temperature	Fahrenheit	Celsius	Gas mark
slightly warm	200	100	¼
slightly warmer	250	120	½
medium	350	180	4
hot	400	200	5
very hot	450	230	8

Wine pairing suggestions

Wine pairing suggestions are shown in a box like this.
If wine is used to prepare a dish, serve that one with the meal.

North of Southwest

Arriba! Arriba!
Chocolate for everyone!

Chocolate tacos to start

Chocolate tacos

Chile unrellenos with jicama slaw and black velvet beans

———————

Layers of flavor

Cocoa-dusted buñuelos with caramelized peaches and dulce de leche

Layered tortilla omelet

———————

Combination plate #3: tamales and lasagna?

Chocolate papaya tamales with mango mint salsa

Breakfast budin (a.k.a. Mexican green lasagna)

———————

Tequila and corn lickin' good

Margarita tapioca

Fresh corn roulade

CHOCOLATE TACOS

While chocolate tacos may sound decadent, this is actually a no-cholesterol recipe. The dark, crisp chocolate tortilla provides a textural and flavor contrast to the sweetness of ripe, fresh fruit. My husband John's favorite food groups are pasta, pizza and hot dogs, and I can even get him to eat fruit when it's surrounded by chocolate and topped with an icy smooth fruit sorbet!

Serves 8

Chocolate tortilla ingredients

½ cup flour

½ cup sugar

3 tablespoons cocoa powder

2 egg whites

¼ cup vegetable oil

⅓ cup skim milk

1½ teaspoons vanilla

¼ teaspoon salt

⅛ teaspoon cayenne pepper

⅛ teaspoon cinnamon

TO MAKE THE BATTER

Place all of the ingredients in a mixing bowl and beat until smooth with an electric mixer. Cover the batter and place it in the refrigerator to chill for at least 2 hours or overnight.

TO COOK AND SHAPE THE TORTILLA

Remove the batter from the refrigerator and allow it to come to room temperature, which will take 20–30 minutes. Heat a small skillet or crepe pan over low heat. Pour in a little less than ¼ cup of batter (I use a long-handled measuring cup as my ladle) and tilt the pan quickly to spread the batter into a 6-inch circle. Once the edges look dry (2 or 3 minutes), loosen the edges with a knife and turn over the tortilla. Cook for another minute or two.

Lift the soft hot chocolate tortilla out of the pan with a knife or spatula and quickly drape it over a rolling pin. It will become firm and crisp as it cools. Alternatively, if you have a taco rack, put the soft tortilla in that to firm up, teasing the middle open so that you'll have lots of room for fruit.

Hint: If the tortilla doesn't firm up, it means it isn't thoroughly done, so cook it a bit longer. It should be dry when you remove it from the skillet.

Fruit alternatives

The list provided is not sacred. Use a variety of whatever is wonderful and fresh at the market. Some alternatives:

- Sliced peaches (grate some nutmeg over them)
- Fresh figs, quartered
- Kumquats, halved
- Mandarin oranges, peeled and sectioned
- Seedless grapes
- Papaya, peeled and sliced

Sweetening strawberries

If your strawberries are not especially sweet, bring out their flavor by tossing 2 tablespoons of balsamic vinegar with the sliced berries. Let them sit for half an hour and the vinegar will bring out the flavor.

Night owl instructions

The tortillas could be made the night before and kept in an airtight container so they don't lose their crispness.

FRESH FRUIT FILLING

2 pints strawberries, hulled and sliced (grind a small bit of fresh black pepper on top)
1 cup raspberries
1 cup blackberries
½ cup blueberries
1 mango, peeled and cut into ½-inch cubes or sliced into ½-inch thick strips
2 kiwi, peeled and sliced into rounds
1 banana, peeled and sliced into rounds just before serving to prevent browning

Gently mix berries together in a bowl. Keep the remaining fruit separate until assembling or they'll pick up the colors from the berries.

TO SERVE

½ pint sorbet (use a flavor of one of the fruits)
8 mint sprigs
8 edible flowers

Place a tortilla on a serving plate. Generously fill it with the berries and then tuck in the mango, kiwi and bananas. Add a scoop of sorbet and garnish with mint and an edible flower.

CHILE UNRELLENOS

All of the ingredients of chile rellenos are included in this dish, but assembled as a quiche. I'd planned to serve it on one of our first mornings at Oak Knoll Inn. We were in the midst of unpacking, and my rolling pin to make a quiche crust was nowhere to be found. (This was before I learned the trick of using a wine bottle for a rolling pin – and we always have plenty of those!) There was filo dough in the refrigerator, so an un-quiche quiche was created. Now I don't use anything else for the crust as the filo provides a contrasting crunch and removes more than half of the calories that are in the traditional crust. Of course, there are still a few in the cheesy-cream filling, but you take opportunities where you get them.

Delicious served bubbling hot out of the oven as part of this Southwestern menu, it can also be served for lunch at room temperature with a lightly dressed green salad.

7 fresh poblano, Anaheim or California chiles (see note)

7 eggs

1 pint heavy cream

1 teaspoon salt

1 teaspoon cumin seeds

16 sheets of filo dough (9 x 13-inch)

2 tablespoons butter, melted

2 tablespoons vegetable or canola oil

1¼ pounds Sonoma or Monterey Jack cheese, cut into ½-inch cubes

¼ cup freshly grated Parmesan or hard, aged Sonoma or Monterey Jack cheese

TO PREPARE CHILES

Grill chiles, turning with tongs until the skin is blackened on all sides. (This can be done on a grill, or directly over the flame on a gas stove, or in a cast iron skillet over medium-high heat, or on a sheet pan under the broiler.) Place the blackened chiles in a bowl and cover the bowl with plastic wrap until the chiles are cool enough to handle. The steam from the hot chiles will loosen their charred skins so you can peel them. Discard seeds and membrane. Tear chiles into 1-inch or narrower strips.

Note: *If time is short or you live in a fresh chile-deprived area, you can skip this step and substitute canned whole green chiles. You'll probably need two 4-ounce cans. Rinse and dry the chiles to remove the canned taste.*

TO ASSEMBLE

Preheat oven to 450°.

Place the eggs, cream and salt in a mixing bowl and beat until thoroughly combined. Toast the cumin seeds in a skillet over medium-high heat for a minute or two until they release their aroma. Add them to the egg/cream mixture.

Mix the melted butter and oil in a small bowl. Brush a light coating on a 9 x 13-inch rectangular glass dish. Place a layer of filo on the bottom of the dish and brush with the butter/oil mixture. Continue with three more layers. Cover the filo with the cubed and grated cheeses, scatter the chile strips over the cheese and then pour in the egg/cream mixture.

Top with the remaining 12 layers of filo, brushing with the butter/oil mixture between each layer. Do not brush the top.

To make it easier to cut after baking, score the filo into serving pieces by cutting through 6 or 7 layers, but not all the way through to the filling or the filo will get soggy. Make one scoring cut the long way and three the short way to create eight pieces.

Place the dish in a preheated 450° oven and bake for 20 minutes. Reduce the heat to 350° and bake for an additional 25–30 minutes. Test by inserting a knife in the middle of the quiche. If the knife comes out clean, it's done. Let it sit for 5 minutes before cutting.

Working with filo

Unless you're lucky enough to have a Middle Eastern shop near you that stocks it fresh, filo can generally be found in the frozen food section of most supermarkets. Leave it in the package and defrost it overnight in the refrigerator. If kept tightly wrapped, it will last for weeks in the refrigerator. There's usually enough to make this recipe two times with some left over.

To prevent filo from drying out as you work with it, keep the unused portion covered with a piece of waxed paper.

Night owl instructions

Prepare the chiles and keep them in the refrigerator in a covered container.
You can also dice and grate the cheeses in advance.

Wine suggestions
Sauvignon Blanc; Chardonnay, non-buttery or heavily oaked

JICAMA SLAW

The crunchy, chilled jicama-cucumber-hot pepper combination provides a contrast in flavor, texture, temperature and piquancy to the hot, smooth quiche and beans.

1 medium-sized jicama, peeled and grated on the large holes of a box grater

½ cup diced peeled cucumber (¼-inch dice), large seeds removed and discarded

1 minced jalapeño or serrano chile (remove seeds and membranes if you like less heat)

¼ cup sweet red pepper, diced

2 tablespoons finely sliced red onion

¼ cup finely chopped fresh cilantro leaves and stems

Juice from ½ lemon

1 tablespoon sour cream

½ cup aioli (see *Pantry,* page 269) or mayonnaise to moisten

Salt and freshly ground pepper to taste

Mix all of the vegetables together in a bowl. Sprinkle with the lemon juice and chill in the refrigerator for at least 20 minutes to let the flavors combine. Mix in the sour cream and aioli or mayonnaise. Salt and pepper just before serving. Use a slotted spoon to serve the slaw so some of the liquid drains away. Garnish with a cilantro sprig.

"I have this theory that chocolate slows down the aging process ... It may not be true, but do I dare take the chance?"

BLACK VELVET BEANS

Beans have a reputation for producing a certain subsequent antisocial behavior. Epazote is a distinctively flavored herb that counteracts that tendency. It grows easily in the garden or in a pot, and according to Diana Kennedy, doyenne of Mexican cooking, it also grows wild in Central Park in New York City. We put in a plant years ago and just wait every spring to see where it will show up this year. The birds scatter the seeds when the herb flowers. Dried epazote is available in gourmet shops or through the mail (see *Resources*). Epazote is not necessary for the success of this recipe, but it will definitely contribute to your reputation as a thoughtful host or hostess.

½ pound dried black beans, sorted to remove any small stones, and rinsed in water
1 small white onion, coarsely chopped (½ cup)
2 cloves garlic, peeled and smashed
1 large sprig fresh epazote or 1½ teaspoons dried (optional)
1 tablespoon fresh thyme or 1 teaspoon dried
1 serrano chile, stem removed or ½ teaspoon dried cayenne
Water to cover

½ teaspoon salt to taste after cooking
1 tablespoon balsamic vinegar
Sour cream to garnish

Night owl instructions

Make the beans ahead and refrigerate them the night before. To reheat, warm 2 tablespoons of vegetable oil in a medium saucepan over medium heat. Add the puréed beans and heat them almost to a boil, stirring occasionally so that they don't stick.

Place all ingredients except salt, vinegar and sour cream in a large saucepan. Cover the beans with cold water to 1 inch over the top. Discard any beans that float.

Bring to a boil and immediately turn the heat down to a simmer. Place the lid on the pot so that it's slightly askew, allowing some steam to escape. Cook for 2–3 hours until the beans are tender. The time varies considerably depending on how dry or old the beans are. Add boiling water as necessary to keep the beans covered.

Drain the beans, reserving a cup of the liquid bean juice. Pour the beans and liquid into a blender, add salt and balsamic vinegar and purée until smooth. Serve with a swirl of sour cream as a garnish.

"There's nothing better than a good friend, except a good friend with chocolate."
Linda Grayson

COCOA-DUSTED BUÑUELOS with CARAMELIZED PEACHES and DULCE de LECHE

This is a quick variation of the buñuelos typically eaten in Oaxaca, Mexico, on Christmas Eve. They're served on broken or irregular pieces of pottery which are then dashed in the street for good luck in the next year. We serve ours instead with a decadent combination of caramelized peaches and dulce de leche. The only thing broken when eating these is the occasional new year's resolution.

Serves 4

Buñuelos ingredients

¾ cup granulated sugar

2 teaspoons unsweetened cocoa powder

1 teaspoon cinnamon

Canola or vegetable oil for deep-frying

4 six-inch flour tortillas

Caramelized peach ingredients

4 peaches, peeled and sliced

½ cup orange juice

3 tablespoons butter

3 tablespoons dark brown sugar

2 tablespoons cognac or brandy

4 scoops of peach sorbet or substitute peach or vanilla ice cream

Wine suggestions
Brut Rosé; Cremant Sparkling Wine

TO MAKE THE BUÑUELOS

Mix sugar, cocoa and cinnamon in a bowl large enough to hold a tortilla.

Heat 2 inches of oil in a skillet over medium-high heat until it reaches 350° on a deep-fry thermometer. Carefully slip a tortilla into the oil. It will puff up dramatically. Once it turns golden brown, turn it over with long-handled tongs to crisp the other side. Remove it to a piece of paper towel placed over several layers of newspaper to absorb any excess oil. Then dip the warm tortilla into the sugar/cocoa, spooning the mixture over both sides to coat the tortilla. Repeat with the other tortillas.

TO CARAMELIZE THE PEACHES

Toss the sliced peaches in a bowl with the orange juice, which will help to keep them from browning. Melt the butter over medium-high heat in a skillet large enough to hold the fruit. Add the brown sugar and stir until it dissolves. Drain the orange juice from the peaches into the skillet and bring to a boil. Add the cognac and continue to boil for 5 minutes until the sauce reduces and thickens. Then add the peaches, stirring to coat them with the liquid. Cook for another minute and then remove from the heat.

TO ASSEMBLE

Serve the buñuelo in a bowl with ¼ of the peach mixture. Add a scoop of sorbet and drizzle dulce de leche on top.

DULCE de LECHE
Caramel sauce (literally, sweet from milk)

For someone who's been accused of starting most recipes with "and first we plant the garden…" I have to confess to a guilty fascination with goofy recipes that call for strange ingredients or cooking methods. The collection includes Coca-Cola cake, mock-apple pie made with Ritz crackers, mayonnaise chocolate cake and others that have been around since food rationing during World War II. But who was it that first thought of poaching a salmon in the dishwasher, or cooking a roast on the car's engine block en route to Grandma's house? And what were they drinking?

A friend from Bolivia gave me this very cherished family recipe, which he would prepare when his brother was coming for a visit after work. He would start the water boiling when he got up to make coffee. By the time he'd had a shower, eaten breakfast, walked the dog and read the paper, it was done. When he and his brother came home from the office, they'd both grab spoons and sit on the back porch, enjoying the dulce and solving the problems of the world.

One 14-ounce can of condensed milk

Place the can in a saucepan and cover it with water. Bring the water to a boil over high heat and then reduce to a gentle simmer. If water evaporates and the top of the can starts peeking through, add more boiling water. After 3 hours, turn off the heat. Once the water has cooled down, open the can and enjoy.

For safety's sake: It's important to keep the can covered with water and not to let all of the water evaporate. For this reason, despite my friend's instructions, I wouldn't go for a walk with the dog while the can (or anything else, for that matter) is on the stove. Should all of the water boil away, the can could overheat and burst – spraying molten caramel everywhere.

LAYERED TORTILLA OMELET

This is one of Shirlee Quick's specialties. The self-professed Chile Queen of Oak Knoll Inn, she often prepares spicy treats for our evening wine and cheese party, and credits Mark Miller, whom she worked with at the Fourth Street Grill in Berkeley, as her chile mentor. On joining us years ago, Shirlee introduced me to the idea of a "pajama day" when she started preparing breakfast once a week so that I could stay in bed with a good book and several kitties. And when I'm truly lucky, she sends me some of this wonderful breakfast on a tray.

Serves 4 to 6

9 large eggs
1½ teaspoons salt and a few turns of freshly ground pepper
1 teaspoon thyme
1 teaspoon oregano
½ teaspoon butter
¾ cup chopped scallions
4 eight-inch flour tortillas
2 cups red chile sauce (recipe follows) or you can purchase green or red chile or enchilada sauce
1 cup cream cheese (even better, use queso fresco if you can get it)
4 ounces goat cheese
1 cup grated Monterey or Sonoma Jack cheese

Night owl instructions

The night before, prepare the sauce and grate the cheese. Mix the goat cheese and cream cheese. Place each in a closed container in the refrigerator overnight and bring to room temperature in the morning. I don't recommend making the omelets ahead as they will dry out. And if you try to assemble the whole dish the night before, the tortillas will become soggy.

TO MAKE THE OMELETS

Preheat oven to 250°. Grease a baking sheet, spread 3 of the tortillas on the sheet and place in the oven to get warm.

Beat the eggs with the salt, pepper and herbs in a quart-sized glass measuring cup to make it easier to divide the eggs in three parts.

Mix the cream cheese and goat cheese together.

Melt ½ teaspoon of butter over medium heat in a skillet the same size as the tortillas. Pour in ⅓ of the egg mixture. Cook until the edges get dry, which will only take a few minutes. Then lift out the flat omelet with a large spatula and place it directly onto a flour tortilla on the warmed greased baking sheet. Repeat two more times, keeping the omelets warm in the oven until the last one is ready.

TO ASSEMBLE

On the baking sheet, ladle ¼ of the sauce over a tortilla/omelet and crumble ⅓ of the cream cheese mixture and ¼ of the jack cheese over the sauce. Sprinkle ⅓ of the scallions on top.

Place the next tortilla/omelet on top and repeat. Repeat again with the third tortilla/omelet and place the remaining plain tortilla on top with the last of the sauce. Sprinkle the remaining jack cheese over the top.

Increase the oven temperature to 350°.

Make a tent out of aluminum foil so that you can cover the stack without touching the top, or all of the cheese will stick and come off on the foil. Bake at 350° for 15 minutes until the tortillas and omelets are heated through and the cheese melts. Remove from the oven and let the stack sit for a few minutes so that the layers don't slide. Cut it into wedges and serve.

1–2 tablespoons olive oil

1 medium onion, coarsely chopped

1 tablespoon Dijon mustard

¼ cup chile powder (mix New Mexico and California chile powders, if available)

½ cup beer (Corona or XX Mexican beer would be appropriate, or substitute sparkling wine or a lively white wine)

1 teaspoon soy sauce

1 teaspoon oregano

1 teaspoon ground cumin

10–12 ripe plum tomatoes or 1½ cans of fire-roasted tomatoes

¼ cup red chile purée (see *Pantry*, page 268) or substitute canned red chile sauce

2 teaspoons balsamic vinegar (or to taste)

Salt and pepper to taste

Wine suggestions
Cabernet Franc; Rioja

RED CHILE SAUCE

In a saucepan, sauté onion in a little bit of olive oil until soft. Add mustard and chile powder. Cook for a few minutes to soften the rawness of the chile powder. Stir in beer, soy sauce, oregano and cumin along with the tomatoes. Cook over medium heat for 20 minutes. Add more beer if the mixture looks dry. Remove the pan from the heat. Let the mixture cool a few minutes and then purée.

Return to a low heat and add the chile purée and balsamic vinegar. Cook a few minutes more to marry the ingredients together. Add more of the beer if needed for a good spreading consistency.

CHOCOLATE PAPAYA TAMALES with MANGO MINT SALSA

Of Mexican heritage, Maria Hernandez is one of my favorite kitchen helpers. The first time I served chocolate tamales, she took one look, and said "CHOCOLATE tamales? And they're too small." Her look said "Is nothing sacred?" Relenting slightly, she told of sweet tamales her mother made with raisins in the masa dough, which inspired the addition of the dried cranberries. When she brought all of the plates back from the dining room completely empty, she said "See. I told you they were too small."

Makes 24 small tamales – serves 8

Tamale dough ingredients

- **½ cup dried cranberries, roughly chopped and marinated overnight in**
- **½ cup tequila**
- **2 egg whites**
- **¼ cup sugar**
- **1 cup milk**
- **1 teaspoon vanilla**
- **4 tablespoons butter**
- **⅔ cup flour, sieved**
- **¼ teaspoon salt**
- **½ teaspoon cinnamon**
- **4 egg yolks, one at a time**
- **3 ounces bittersweet chocolate, melted**

TO MAKE THE TAMALE DOUGH

Drain the marinated cranberries through a sieve. Set aside the by now beautifully flavored tequila for the salsa. Add the vanilla to the milk in a small saucepan and bring to a simmer over medium-high heat.

Beat egg whites with a mixer on medium-high. Once they start to thicken and become opaque, add the sugar and continue beating until the whites form soft peaks when the beaters are lifted.

In a medium saucepan, melt the butter. Mix the flour, salt and cinnamon and stir into the melted butter with a wooden spoon. Add the warm vanilla/milk all at once and stir enthusiastically until the lumps disappear. Add one egg yolk, stirring until it's thoroughly incorporated and the mixture loses its shine. Continue adding yolks one by one. Stir in the melted chocolate and the drained cranberries.

Stir about a quarter of the egg whites into the chocolate mixture. This loosens it up so that it will be easier to fold in the remaining whites gently until no white is visible.

Tamale wrap ingredients

24 corn husks

24 2 x ¾-inch slices of peeled and seeded papaya

24 foot-long pieces of raffia, or use strips of corn husk

Mango mint salsa ingredients

1 mango, peeled and cut into ¼-inch dice

½ cup fresh pineapple, diced

2 kiwi, peeled and diced

½ cup cantaloupe, diced

½ cup honeydew melon, diced

½ cup red onion, diced

1 small jalapeño chile, seeded and finely chopped

1 habañero chile, seeded and finely chopped (optional – not for sissies)

2 tablespoons fresh lime juice

1 teaspoon sugar

½ cup tequila used to marinate cranberries for tamales

¼ cup finely chopped fresh mint leaves

½ teaspoon salt, or more to taste

TO WRAP THE TAMALE

Soften corn husks in warm water for 20–30 minutes until they're pliable. Drain. Open a husk with the pointy end at the top. Spread 3 tablespoons of dough into a 4-inch square in the middle, leaving a border all around. Put the papaya slice in the middle. Pick up the left and right sides of the corn husk and bring them together, which will fold the husk in half, enclosing the papaya completely. Roll the border on these long sides together to seal, with the seam facing up. Fold the top (pointy) and bottom ends underneath and tie the bundle like a present with a piece of raffia.

Stack the tamales in a steamer in a criss-cross fashion so that the steam can flow around them. Place any extra husks over the top. Place the pot lid on tightly and steam the tamales over boiling water for 20 minutes. Remove from heat for 10 minutes before serving.

TO PREPARE THE MANGO MINT SALSA

Place all ingredients in a medium bowl and toss gently to combine.

TO ASSEMBLE

8 slices of star fruit

8 slices of banana, grilled

8 strawberries

mango sorbet

8 mint sprigs

Place a mound of salsa in the center of the plate. Unwrap two tamales and lean them on the salsa. Leave the third one wrapped – everyone loves a present. Garnish with a small scoop of sorbet, the pieces of fruit and a mint sprig.

Wine suggestion
A young fruity Rhone varietal such as the Stags Leap Winery Petite Sirah or a balanced fruity Pinot Noir from Merry Edwards stand up to all of the flavors. Or try an icy chilled sparkling wine for contrast: Domaine Carneros late disgorged Brut, Schramsberg Blanc de Noir, Domaine Chandon Rosé Etoile or Gloria Ferrar Carneros Cuve.

BREAKFAST BUDIN
(a.k.a. Mexican green lasagna)

One winter morning as Maria was serving breakfast, a guest asked her for her favorite Oak Knoll breakfast. She said, "Barbara's Mexican green lasagna." It got that name when we had an Italian guest who wanted to know what we'd just served him. I usually make this with fresh tomatillos from the garden, but as a result of Maria volunteering it for breakfast in January, I know that canned tomatillos can be substituted.

Serves 8

2–4 tablespoons vegetable oil for frying
24 small fresh corn tortillas (4-inch)

Eggs ingredients

12 eggs, beaten
½ teaspoon salt
A grinding of fresh pepper
1 tablespoon cumin seeds
2 tablespoons olive or vegetable oil

Rajas ingredients

7 poblano or Anaheim chiles, roasted
   and peeled (see page 27 under
   ***Chile unrellenos*)**
¼ cup vegetable oil
¼ cup onion, thinly sliced
½ teaspoon salt, or to taste
2 tablespoons olive or vegetable oil

Tomatillo sauce ingredients
(makes 2 cups)

2 cups tomatillos, husk removed
2 cloves garlic
½ teaspoon salt
½ cup reserved water

TO PREPARE THE TORTILLAS

Heat the oil in a small frying pan and fry each tortilla for a few seconds, turning once. They should still be soft. Drain them on a paper towel placed over newspapers.

TO PREPARE THE EGGS

Beat the eggs with the salt and pepper. Place a medium-sized skillet over medium-high heat and add the cumin seeds. Shake the pan so that the seeds toast and don't burn. When they start to release their aroma, add the oil and turn the heat down to low. Add the eggs. Stir them and scramble lightly until still very soft and loose. They'll finish cooking in the oven.

TO PREPARE THE RAJAS

Remove the stems, seeds and veins and cut the chiles into ½-inch strips that are 2 inches long. In a small frying pan, heat the oil and sauté the onions gently until they're soft but not brown. Add the sliced chiles and salt, cover and cook over low heat for 6–8 minutes until tender.

TO PREPARE THE TOMATILLO SAUCE

Put the tomatillos in a saucepan and cover them with water. Bring to a boil, turn down the heat and simmer for 10–15 minutes until the tomatillos lose their bright green color and turn soft. Drain them, reserving ½ cup of the water.

Put the tomatillos and the rest of the ingredients in a blender and purée until smooth. Lightly coat a small frying pan with oil and add the sauce. Cook over medium-high heat for about 10 minutes until thickened.

TO ASSEMBLE

Preheat the oven to 375°.

Grease an ovenproof dish or springform pan 3–4 inches deep and 10 inches across. Use 6 tortillas to cover the bottom, tearing a couple of them into pieces to fill in the spaces.

Spread ⅓ cup sour cream over the tortilllas. Sprinkle ⅓ of the scrambled eggs on top, then ⅓ of the rajas and ¼ of the cheese. Ladle ½ cup of the tomatillo sauce on top. Repeat twice more, ending with tortillas on top and the remaining cheese. Bake for 30 minutes until the cheese is melted and slightly toasted. Let it sit for about 10 minutes before slicing like a pie.

Note: *If time is short or ingredients hard to come by, substitute a canned green enchilada sauce for the tomatillo sauce and use canned green chiles (drained and rinsed off with water) in the rajas. As an alternative, serve it with a lightly dressed fresh green salad for a hearty vegetarian luncheon.*

Ingredients to assemble

1 cup sour cream

2 cups grated mild cheddar or Monterey or Sonoma Jack cheese, or a combination

Wine suggestions
Chardonnay, non-oaky; Cabernet Sauvignon, fruity not high-alcohol; Merlot

tequila and corn lickin' good

MARGARITA TAPIOCA

serves 8

Tapioca ingredients

¾ cup instant tapioca

1¼ cups sugar

½ teaspoon salt

5 egg yolks

3 cups milk

1 cup half-and-half

Zest of one lime (remove the zest before the juice)

¼ cup lime juice

½ cup tequila

Serving ingredients

1 tablespoon cocoa

¼ cup sugar

½ teaspoon sea salt

1 pint of sliced strawberries (or substitute other sweet berries, diced fresh mango, papaya or grilled pineapple)

Chocolate tequila lime sorbet (see *Frozen Delights*, page 261)

TO MAKE THE TAPIOCA

Combine the tapioca, sugar, salt, yolks, milk and half-and-half in the top of a double boiler. Cook for 15–20 minutes over boiling water until the mixture thickens, stirring occasionally with a whisk. Remove the pan from the heat and put the tapioca in a bowl to let it cool.

Stir the lime zest, juice and tequila into the cooled tapioca. Cover the bowl and refrigerate for at least an hour (or overnight if that works better with your schedule) so that the flavors have time to get acquainted.

TO SERVE

Remove the tapioca from the refrigerator 30 minutes before serving.

Mix the sugar, cocoa and salt on a saucer or flat-bottomed bowl. Moisten the edge of a margarita glass with a cut lime. Dip the edge into the cocoa mixture.

Spoon ½ cup of the tapioca into the margarita glass and top with fruit and a scoop of chocolate lime tequila sorbet.

Note: *If you'd prefer to do without the alcohol, heat the tequila on top of the stove in a small sauté pan until very warm. Once warm, pull the pan towards you and tilt it towards the flame. It should ignite. BE CAREFUL. DO NOT STAND OVER THE PAN or you'll be serving breakfast minus your eyebrows.*

FRESH CORN ROULADE

Serves 4

Soufflé base ingredients

¼ cup sweet butter

5 tablespoons flour

5 eggs

1½ cups milk, at room temperature or warmed slightly

½ teaspoon salt

Pinch of cayenne

½ cup freshly grated Parmesan

TO PREPARE THE SOUFFLÉ BASE

Preheat oven to 400°.

Separate the eggs, placing the whites in a large (preferably copper) mixing bowl. Beat the yolks slightly in a small bowl and put aside.

Melt the butter in a saucepan. Add the flour and whisk constantly over medium heat until you've created a smooth, lightly colored roux. Add the milk all at once and continue stirring until the mixture thickens and coats the whisk. Remove the pan from the heat and whisk in cayenne and salt.

Whisk a tablespoon or so of the hot milk mixture into the yolks, then another, then another until you've warmed the yolks. (If you add it all at once, you'll have lumpy scrambled eggs.) Then add the warmed yolks to the rest of the milk mixture in the pan and whisk together until smooth.

Add a pinch of salt to the egg whites and beat them until stiff. Mix about a third of the whites and ¼ cup of the Parmesan into the yolks to loosen them up so they'll mix more easily. Then fold this yolk mixture gently into the remaining whites.

Line a cookie sheet or jelly roll pan with parchment. To make it easier to move and roll the soufflé, butter the parchment and sprinkle flour on top, shaking the pan to cover the entire surface. Discard any extra loose flour. You could substitute a silicone sheet for the parchment, but will still need to butter and flour it or the soufflé will stick.

Pour the egg mixture onto the pan and sprinkle the remaining ¼ cup of Parmesan over the top. Bake for 15 minutes. It will swell up as it cooks and then flatten out after you remove it from the oven and it cools. Let it sit for a few minutes while you prepare the filling.

Corn filling ingredients

1–2 tablespoons olive oil
2–3 ears of corn
1 cup sweet red pepper, diced
¾ cup scallions, chopped
Oregano to taste
Salt and pepper

½ cup grated pepper jack cheese

Night owl instructions

Prepare and bake the soufflé the night before. After it has cooled down, wrap the pan in plastic wrap and keep it in the refrigerator. You can also prepare the filling, but don't spread it on the soufflé until just before baking or the whole thing will get soggy. In the morning, pull the soufflé and filling out of the refrigerator half an hour before assembling. Bake at 350° for 15 minutes to get the cheese to melt and everything heated through.

Wine suggestions
Rosé; Fume Blanc

TO PREPARE THE CORN FILLING

Put olive oil in a skillet over medium heat. Remove corn kernels from the cob and sauté them with the peppers until they soften. Season with salt, pepper and oregano. Remove from the heat and add scallions.

TO ASSEMBLE

Preheat oven to 300°.

Spread the corn filling over the roulade and grate the cheese over the entire surface.

Starting on the long side, use the parchment paper to help you roll the soufflé into a long firm cylinder. Center the roulade on the parchment on the cookie sheet and place it in a low oven for 10 minutes or so, until the cheese melts. Let it sit for a few minutes before cutting it into twelve 1-inch slices which showcase the beautiful spiral. Overlap three slices per plate.

Note: *This can also be served at room temperature. It makes unusual picnic fare, served with a tossed green salad.*

Alternative: *There is no end of fillings for this roulade. Make any salsa-type filling. Sauté some onions and garlic in a bit of olive oil. Take off the heat and mix with chopped tomatoes, minced cilantro, chopped scallions, avocado, even mango – whatever you like in a salsa. Or use ricotta and a mix of bitter greens (perhaps sautéed chard) with chopped walnuts, cream cheese (and a little goat cheese mixed in) with a thick reduction of chopped tomatoes and basil.*

Asian Persuasion

You will have a prosperous life and eat plenty of chocolate

With omelet you get eggroll

Apple eggroll
Lacy Singapore omelet
Chocolate fortune cookies

Summer on the Pacific Rim

Two melons summer soup with white chocolate grapes
Summer vegetable ricepaper roll over Chinese long beans

APPLE EGGROLL

Makes 8 eggrolls

Apple eggroll ingredients

2 tart apples (Granny Smith, Pippin...
    not Delicious) peeled, cored and
    minced
½ cup sweet golden raisins, minced
1 scallion, minced
1 teaspoon freshly grated ginger
1 teaspoon cinnamon
1 teaspoon freshly grated nutmeg
3 tablespoons brown sugar
8 eggroll wrappers
Powdered sugar to dust the finished
    eggrolls

Dipping sauce ingredients

2 tablespoons butter
2 tablespoons brown sugar
1 teaspoon freshly grated ginger
1 glass of Champagne – ⅔ cup
3 kiwi, peeled and chopped finely
Freshly ground white pepper
½ teaspoon hot red pepper flakes
    (we use a garden mixture that
    includes cayenne, red bonnet,
    habañero and jalapeño)
2 tablespoons soy sauce

Wine suggestion
Late harvest Chenin Blanc

TO MAKE THE EGGROLLS

Heat 2 inches of oil to 350° in a deep skillet.

Mix everything except the eggroll wrappers and powdered sugar.
(If you don't like all of the chopping and mincing, pulse the ingredients
in a food processor.)

Place an eggroll wrapper on your work surface with one of the corners
pointing towards you. Pile a large spoonful (about ¼ cup) of the filling
in the upper half triangle of the wrapper. Moisten the edges of the
wrapper with a brush dipped in water. Fold the top corner over the
filling, then fold in the sides and roll. The filling should be completely
encased. Continue with the remaining wrappers.

Carefully place each eggroll in the hot oil and deep fry, first on
one side, then the other until crispy and golden brown. Dust with
powdered sugar on the top only and serve with the dipping sauce.

TO MAKE THE SPICY KIWI DIPPING SAUCE

Melt butter in a small saucepan. Stir in sugar until it melts and begins
to caramelize. Add ginger and a glass of Champagne. Reduce over
medium heat for 10 minutes. Add kiwi, white pepper, red pepper flakes
and soy sauce. Simmer for 10 minutes and serve.

LACY SINGAPORE OMELET

Singapore is known among food-lovers for the delicious variety of its street food. This omelet can be found wrapping all sorts of fillings from vegetables to shrimp or chicken. In Singapore, they use a tool that looks like a can with holes punched in the bottom of it, but lacking that, I've found that a sieve works beautifully, as does a squirt bottle of the type found filled with mustard at a hot dog stand.

Serves 4

Omelet ingredients

5 eggs

Spray oil for skillet

Filling ingredients

1 tablespoon oil

⅓ cup finely chopped onion

2 scallions, sliced into ½-inch pieces

½ pound shiitake mushrooms, stems removed and sliced into ¼-inch pieces

½ cup sweet red bell pepper, diced

1 tablespoon freshly grated gingerroot (or substitute 1 teaspoon ground ginger)

1 serrano chile, finely minced

Juice from ½ lime

1 tablespoon soy sauce

1 tablespoon hot chili oil

Wine suggestions
Dry Riesling; Gewurztraminer

Crack the eggs into a bowl and beat them until they're smooth. Set aside while you prepare the omelet filling.

TO PREPARE THE FILLING

Heat the oil in a skillet (or wok) over medium heat. Add the onions and sauté until they start to turn translucent. Turn up the heat and add the rest of the ingredients, stirring briskly, until the mushrooms turn soft and moist. Take the skillet off the heat while you make the omelets.

TO MAKE THE OMELET

Spray or brush a separate skillet lightly with oil and heat it over medium heat until a drop of water sizzles when you put it in the pan.

Place a large sieve over a bowl. Pour some of the beaten eggs into the sieve. Because the eggs are viscous, they won't all flow right through the sieve in one spot, they'll start coming through in several locations. Hold the sieve over the bowl and bring it to the skillet. Take the bowl away and quickly drizzle the egg in a rough 6–8-inch circle into the skillet. It will look lacy and have holes, but should hold together. (Another option is to put strained eggs into a squirt bottle with a pointy top and rapidly create a lacy shape in the pan. If you don't strain the eggs before putting them in the squirt bottle, the top will clog at an inconvenient moment in mid-squirt.)

The omelet will cook fairly quickly – just a minute should do it. When the edges start to look dry, remove it from the skillet to a plate and make another. You should have enough egg to make at least 8 omelets and a few mistakes.

Place ⅛ of the filling in the omelet and roll it. Serve 2 per person.

CHOCOLATE FORTUNE COOKIES

This is your chance to personalize breakfast with fortunes tailored to your guests or your location. Here in Napa's wine country, we've served one saying, "You will meet a tall, dark handsome stranger…who will pour you wine," followed by "You will meet a short, dumpy stranger…who will pour you wine." We recently had a favorite guest who received a happy birthday call from Hilary Clinton. At breakfast we made a fortune cookie for her that read: "Hilary called to ask us to celebrate your birthday with a bottle of Champagne. So we did."

Makes 12–15 cookies

½ cup flour

½ cup sugar

2 tablespoons cocoa powder

1 teaspoon 5-spice powder

2 egg whites

¼ cup oil

⅓ cup skim milk

1½ teaspoons vanilla

¼ teaspoon salt

12–15 really good fortunes printed on strips of paper

Sift the flour, sugar, cocoa and 5-spice powder together. Add the remaining ingredients and mix thoroughly. Let the batter rest for half an hour.

Preheat oven to 400°. Place a silicone sheet on a cookie sheet. Ladle 2 tablespoons of batter onto the sheet. Spread the batter with the bottom of the ladle, making a 3-inch circle. Repeat so that you have four future cookies. (If you get ambitious and make any more at one time, it will be hard to handle them quickly enough when they come out of the oven. Practice first with 2. There's plenty of batter to allow a few mistakes.)

Bake for 6 minutes. Remove one cookie at a time and fold it around the fortune. The cookie will firm up as it cools. Repeat with the other cookies. As you get comfortable with this you can have 2 cookie sheets going.

HOW TO FOLD A FORTUNE COOKIE

Practice with a piece of paper. It's not difficult to do, just difficult to describe.

Working quickly, with a spatula remove a cookie from the baking sheet and invert it onto a work surface. Put a fortune in the middle of the cookie and hold it in place with your index fingers. Softly fold the cookie in half, keeping your fingers in place so that you don't crease the bottom edge of what is now a semicircle. Use your thumbnail to make a dent in the middle of that bottom edge and gently fold the cookie in half, bringing together the edges where your index fingers are.

TWO MELONS SUMMER SOUP with WHITE CHOCOLATE GRAPES

All of this can be made the night before, so on a warm summer morning there's no need to heat up the stove or turn on the oven. Just serve, add a splash of Midori (or not) to a glass of sparkling wine and retire to a table in the shade and dine to the music of birdsong.

Serves 6

1 cantaloupe or charentais melon

2 tablespoons sugar

Juice from 1 lemon

½ cup Champagne or sparkling wine

Pinch of salt

1 honeydew melon

Juice from 1 lime

¼ cup Midori melon liqueur

A grating of nutmeg

2–3 ounces white chocolate

30 grapes – green or red seedless

Remove the seeds from the cantaloupe, extract a dozen melon balls with a melon-baller, small ice cream scoop or a spoon. Set the balls aside until you're ready to serve. Remove the skin from the melon and put the flesh in a blender or food processor with the remaining ingredients. Purée until well blended with no big chunks of melon remaining, just small bits. Place the soup in a covered container in the refrigerator for at least an hour and preferably overnight.

Repeat the procedure with the honeydew melon.

Melt white chocolate in the top of a double boiler. Pick up each grape with a toothpick and dip it into the chocolate. Stick the toothpick in something firm, like an apple, that will hold the coated grape in the air to dry.

To serve, ladle the thicker soup into one side of a tilted soup bowl. Then ladle the other soup into the other side. Garnish with melon balls and melon sorbet. Serve with the white chocolate grapes.

Alternative: *When stone fruit is ripe, make a variation using white and peach-colored nectarines or peaches. Make the darker fruit soup with 2 tablespoons of Amaretto instead of the Midori.*

SUMMER VEGETABLE RICEPAPER ROLL over CHINESE LONG BEANS

Summer rolls are made with ricepaper and can be filled with anything, at any time of the year. But summer rolls in the summer filled with summer vegetables just seems right. They're light, don't require much stove-time, and can be filled with chilled vegetables as well as hot.

Serves 6

2 bunches of Chinese long beans
2 tablespoons olive oil
1 tablespoon rice vinegar, for the beans
Salt and freshly ground pepper to taste

2 tablespoons vegetable oil
½ cup sliced red onion
1 pound shiitake (stems removed) and/
    or porcini mushrooms, sliced
1 serrano or cayenne pepper, seeds and
    membrane removed, then minced
2 tablespoons soy sauce
1 tablespoon rice vinegar, for the
    vegetables
3 baby bok choy, quartered the long
    way, top to bottom
¼ pound pea shoots

12 ricepaper wrappers
¼ cup hoisin or oyster sauce

TO PREPARE THE LONG BEANS

Bring a medium saucepan of water to a boil. Add the beans and simmer for 2 minutes until they turn bright green and become more flexible. Drain the water off and immerse the beans in ice water to stop the cooking. Season with a sprinkling of vegetable oil, rice vinegar, salt and pepper and toss. Arrange on the plate where you'll be serving the rice paper rolls. They can be woven, as illustrated, or rolled into spirals, laid diagonally across the plate, made into a basket or whatever your imagination dictates.

TO PREPARE THE VEGETABLES

Heat the oil in a skillet over medium-high heat. Add the onion, mushrooms and pepper and stir-fry quickly. Stir in the soy sauce and rice vinegar. Add the bok choy, toss quickly for 1–2 minutes and remove the skillet from the heat.

TO SERVE

Have a bowl of warm salted water ready, large enough to hold the ricepaper wrapper. The water should be about body temperature – 100° or so. Slide the wrapper into the water and turn it around until it's softened and flexible. Place the wrapper on a work surface, add sautéed vegetables and pea shoots. Roll and place on the beans. Drizzle with hoisin or oyster sauce and serve 2 per person.

A Little Italy

La Vita with plenty of Dolce

Rainbows in the morning

Fruit pizza

Frittata arrotolata with rainbow chard and pine nuts

Chocolate pasta to start

Chocolate pasta with sautéed strawberries

Breakfast pizza

A side trip to Verona

Spring frittata

Triple-threat chocolate zucchini muffins

Antipasti

Fresh melon with frizzled prosciutto

Chocolate zabaglione

Breakfast in Venice

Chocolate hazelnut biscotti

Harry's grilled salmon with zucchini curry sauce

FRUIT PIZZA

My cousin Devon tells me that she knows she's in trouble when she reads a recipe that starts, "You just…" Well, Cuz, here it is, because the ingredients depend entirely on what fruit is in season. We've prepared 4 seasonal variations, but the alternative possibilities are endless. Pictured are strawberry/rhubarb for spring, blackberry/raspberry/blueberry for summer, pear/kiwi with chocolate nibs for autumn, and blood orange/kumquat for winter. *You just* use what's available, fresh and wonderful in your garden or farmer's market.

Serves 8

Pizza dough ingredients

1½ cups flour

2 teaspoons baking powder

½ teaspoon salt

3 ounces cold sweet butter cut into cubes

½ cup plus 2 tablespoons cold milk

Strawberry sauce ingredients

1 cup strawberries, sliced

¼ cup sugar

2 tablespoons water

Juice from ½ lemon

TO MAKE THE DOUGH

Mix flour, baking powder and salt in a food processor. Add butter and pulse 30 or 35 times until you've created pea-size pieces. Add cold milk and pulse just until combined. There will be small clumps.

Dump the dough out onto your floured work surface. Knead it a few times and roll it out or push and poke the dough into a 12-inch circle. Gently fold it in half or quarters to make it easier to move, and place it on a cookie sheet. Pinch the edge slightly to raise it so it will hold in the sauce and topping.

STRAWBERRY SAUCE

Place all ingredients in a medium saucepan. Bring to a boil. Reduce the heat and cook gently until the berries are mushy, stirring occasionally. This will take about 10 minutes. Blend the berries and let the sauce cool slightly while you prepare the dough. Strain if you'd prefer to get rid of the seeds.

SAUCE ALTERNATIVES

Maple syrup brushed on the dough when using apples and pears.

Lemon curd with citrus (see *Pantry*, page 277, to make your own, or purchase a jar)

Strawberry sauce (recipe above) when strawberries and rhubarb are in season. Or replace the strawberries with raspberries or blackberries. Your imagination is the only limit.

Ingredients to assemble

½ cup of sauce

2 cups of fruit

¼ cup brown sugar

Wine suggestions
Pinot Grigio; Sauvignon Blanc; Rosé;
Johannesberg Riesling

TO ASSEMBLE

Preheat oven to 400°.

Spread sauce over pizza dough. Arrange a ring of sliced fruit around the edge of the pizza, then continue with another type of fruit in concentric rings, working your way to the center until the dough is completely covered. Sprinkle a little brown sugar over the top.

Bake in oven for 20 minutes until the crust is golden. Remove from the oven. Let the pizza cool for 5–10 minutes until the fruit stops running. Slice it into 8 pieces and serve with a wonderful fresh sorbet.

TOPPING CHOICES

2 cups of a combination of whatever fruit is in season: sliced bananas, kiwis, strawberries, blackberries, pitted bing cherries… Use peaches or mango as a topping over raspberry sauce, or fresh figs with prosciutto and gorgonzola…

Hint: When using apples, bananas, pears, peaches or any other fruit that turns brown when exposed to the air, slice the fruit into a bowl with some orange juice or acidulated water (water to which lemon juice or a vitamin C tablet has been added). The ascorbic acid in citrus keeps the fruit from browning.

FRITTATA ARROTOLATA with RAINBOW CHARD and PINE NUTS

Every once in a while, PBS runs a retrospective of old Julia Child shows. If you have a chance to watch her omelet show, don't miss it. In fact, rent it if you can. It's Julia at her best.

She would probably give a skeptical look to the use of a non-stick pan, preferring the traditional French well-seasoned omelet pan. And I know she'd use clarified butter rather than the butter-oil combination I favor. The point of both methods is to be able to cook at higher heat without burning the butter.

When making this dish, I recommend announcing all of your moves with Julia's signature voice. "Now we're melting the butter. People who insist on using margarine are just foolish. A little butter never hurt anyone… Now pour the eggs into the pan…"

Serves 6

1 large bunch of chard in all the colors available
2 tablespoons olive oil
1 clove garlic, finely minced
½ cup pine nuts (optional)
½ cup freshly grated Parmesan or dry jack cheese

1 tablespoon butter
1 tablespoon olive oil
8 eggs
1 teaspoon salt
Freshly ground pepper
A few gratings of nutmeg

Wine suggestions
Pinot Grigio; Sauvignon Blanc

Preheat oven to 350°.

Strip the leaves from the stems of the chard. Chop the stems into ½-inch pieces. Roughly chop the leaves.

Heat the olive oil over medium heat in a frying pan that has a lid. Stir in the stem bits and garlic and cook for a few minutes until softened. Stir in the chard leaves, turn the heat down to low and cover the pan for 3–4 minutes so that the chard wilts. Add the pine nuts and cheese.

Melt the butter and oil in a large, preferably frying pan over medium heat. Beat the eggs with salt and pepper and nutmeg and pour them into the pan. As the edges start to cook and look dry, lift them up with a spatula and let some of the uncooked egg run underneath until the omelet is set.

Spread the chard mixture over the omelet, leaving a ½-inch border. Snuggly roll up the omelet to cover all of the filling and slide it seam-side down onto a greased baking sheet. Bake for 10 minutes, until heated through.

Cut into slices and serve with a lightly dressed salad of mustard, arugala or other bitter greens.

CHOCOLATE PASTA with SAUTÉED STRAWBERRIES

The simple way to match wine to a meal is to use the same wine when preparing the dish. (Adding a glass or two to the cook is helpful as well.) Sangiovese from California, a fruity Chianti from Italy or a young Cabernet Franc are appropriate for a pasta dish. Zinfandel often has a peppery note which echoes the freshly ground pepper on the berries. As with all wine choices, use what you like to drink.

Serves 6

6 ounces dried chocolate pasta (see *Chocoholics* in *Resources,* or make your own with the recipe on the next page)

2 tablespoons butter

2 cups strawberries, hulled and sliced

2 tablespoons brown sugar

¾ cup Sangiovese, Zinfandel or other spicy red wine

½ teaspoon freshly ground pepper, or more to taste

¾ cup whipped cream

¼ cup chocolate nibs

Meyer lemon sorbet

Bring a pot of water to a boil with a teaspoon of salt. Add the pasta and cook al dente, according to the package instructions – generally 5–7 minutes. If you've made your own pasta, it will take even less time. Drain and set aside.

Melt the butter in a skillet over medium-high heat. Add the strawberries and quickly toss. As soon as the berries are coated with butter and start to soften slightly, lift them out with a slotted spoon and put into a bowl.

Add sugar to the pan and stir it around to soak up the butter and juices. When the sugar melts and starts to caramelize, pour in the wine, stir and reduce the sauce over high heat until it's syrupy.

To serve, toss the pasta in the sauce. Divide into six portions. Grind fresh pepper over the strawberries and spoon the berries over the pasta. Top with a dollop of whipped cream, a sprinkling of chocolate nibs and a scoop of Meyer lemon sorbet.

To make whipped cream

1 vanilla bean, halved and soaked overnight in ½ cup cognac (or substitute 1 tablespoon vanilla extract)

1 cup heavy cream

1 tablespoon powdered sugar

1 tablespoon sour cream

Save the cognac to mix with the strawberries, and use a little with the whipped cream at the end.

With a sharp knife, scrape the vanilla bean seeds into the cream in a mixing bowl. Add the powdered sugar and place the bowl and beaters or whisk in the freezer for half an hour.

Whip or whisk the cream vigorously until it thickens but is still soft enough to fall off the beaters when you lift them out of the bowl. Add the sour cream and a tablespoon of the cognac. Whip until the cream is firm enough to hold the shape of the beaters when you lift them, but before it turns into butter. Err on the side of too soft.

CHOCOLATE PASTA

2 cups flour

½ cup cocoa

¼ cup confectioner's sugar

4 eggs

1 teaspoon vanilla

1–2 tablespoons water

Sift the dry ingredients into a mound. Make a well in the middle and add the eggs and vanilla. Use a fork to slowly incorporate the flour mixture in from the edge of the well. Knead with your hands to create a smooth dough. If it's fighting back and you're having trouble working it, add water, a teaspoon at a time. Cover the dough in plastic wrap and let it rest for half an hour.

Roll out the dough to the thickness of spaghetti or fettuccine, using a pasta machine if you have one. Cut the dough into long noodles, ¼-inch wide. Place them on a kitchen towel and let them dry for 2–3 hours.

Note: *If you're not going to use the noodles the same day, place them in an airtight container in the refrigerator.*

"There's more to life than chocolate, but not right now."

BREAKFAST PIZZA

Pizza the morning-after is a New York tradition. Put on the BeeGee's *Saturday Night Fever* sound track, stack two slices on top of each other and strut your stuff like John Travolta. Or seize the opportunity to let your inner Pavarotti emerge. Belt out a little Puccini as you twirl the dough in the air on well-floured hands. It adds joy to the morning, although for first-timers, a rolling pin is a serviceable substitute.

Most home kitchens aren't equipped with a pizza oven or a stone or brick oven insert, which would allow the crust to cook quickly and keep it from getting soggy once all of the topping ingredients are added. To produce a crispy crust with a standard home oven, here we pre-bake it, then top it. As we're lightly pre-baking the crust, the eggs need to be partially done as well. If you don't like poaching eggs, gently and lightly fry them sunny side-up instead.

1 recipe pizza dough (an easy recipe follows or buy ready-made dough)
1 cup tomato sauce – use your favorite spaghetti sauce, preferably home-made
1½ cups shredded fresh mozzarella cheese
1 tablespoon minced fresh basil
1 teaspoon dried oregano
2 sausages – chicken apple, chicken pesto or spicy Italian
8 very fresh eggs
½ cup grated Parmesan
½ teaspoon salt
Freshly ground pepper

TO PREPARE THE CRUST

Preheat oven to 450°

Toss or roll out the pizza dough in a circle to fit your largest baking sheet. If you have a round pizza pan with holes in the bottom, use that. It will help keep the dough crispy. Prick the dough a few times with a fork to keep it from billowing up in the oven. Bake for 8 minutes until very lightly browned. Check the dough after a few minutes. If it is pillowing, just push it back down with a mitt-covered hand.

TO POACH THE EGGS

Fresh eggs hold together best during poaching, so if possible, use eggs you've just purchased from a source you know to be fresh.

Over high heat, bring 3 inches of water to a boil in a medium saucepan and then turn the heat down until the water is just simmering with steam coming off the top and a tiny bubble or two appearing every few seconds. Crack an egg into a small bowl and pour it gently into the simmering water. Repeat with the other eggs. Place them in the water in a clockwise circle to make it easier to remember in which order they'll be done. Undercook the eggs, as they'll finish cooking on the pizza. When the white is almost firm and the yolk is still quite runny, remove each egg with a slotted spoon and put it into a bowl of cold water to stop the cooking until you're ready to assemble the pizza.

TO PREPARE THE SAUSAGES

Place the sausages on a preheated ridged grill pan or a hot skillet over medium-high heat. Cook until the skin gets a slightly blackened char and then turn the sausages over to do the same to the other side. Remove to a cutting board and slice each into 8 pieces, discarding the end bits (or feeding them to the dog).

TO ASSEMBLE

Spread the tomato sauce to within an inch of the edge of the crust. Sprinkle mozzarella over the sauce. Pick up the poached eggs with a slotted spoon and place them on a dish towel for a minute to drain.

Wine suggestions
Grenache-Mouvedre; Sangiovese

Place the eggs evenly around the outside edge of the pizza. Put a slice of sausage between each egg and another below the egg towards the middle of the pizza. Sprinkle with Parmesan, basil and oregano, and season with salt and pepper.

TO BAKE

Place the pizza in the preheated 450° oven for 12–15 minutes until the cheese is melted and bubbly. Slice into 8 wedges and serve with a lightly dressed salad.

Pizza dough

This is easy easy easy and is based on my friend, the chocolate poet, Tony Kruglinski's wet dough method and a similar approach from *Artisan Bread in Five Minutes a Day*, a wonderful book that takes the fuss out of bread making. All of the ingredients are mixed together. No kneading or waiting around is required because the dough goes into the refrigerator until you want it, which can be up to two weeks later.

Makes enough for two pizzas, or several smaller ones

2 packages of yeast (equals ½ ounce)
1½ tablespoons salt
3 cups warm water
6½ cups flour

In a large mixing bowl, add the yeast and salt to warm water. (The water should feel slightly warm to the touch, which would make it 100–105°.) Add all of the flour and mix with a heavy-duty mixer with a dough hook or paddle, or use your hands moistened with water. Once there are no more dry spots and the mixture is uniform, you're done.

Put it in a lidded plastic container 2 to 3 times the size of the dough so there's room for it to rise. Leave the covered container on the counter while you're cleaning up so it gets a headstart and then put it in the refrigerator overnight or until you need it.

When you're ready to make a pizza, cover your hands with flour and scoop out half of the dough, refrigerating the rest for another day. Smooth the dough by turning it around in your hands, running your thumbs over the top and tucking the odd bits underneath. Set it on the counter to rest for half an hour while you prepare all of the topping ingredients.

SPRING FRITTATA

Until after World War II, the typical Italian kitchen didn't have an oven, just a stove top. En route to church on Sunday, mama brought her lasagna or other casserole to the baker, where he put it in his oven, to be picked up on the way home. Frittata, literally a fried omelet, could be cooked at home on top of the stove in a skillet. Traditionally it's left in the pan until nearly done, then flipped over and cooked some more – harsh treatment for a delicate egg mixture. I've been served some beautiful frittatas, but too often there's a slight taste of overcooked egg and a dry texture, and skin has formed on the outside. This garden frittata is halfway to a quiche, as it's only slightly cooked on the stove top and then finished in the oven, allowing it to stay moist and light. And it's more likely to reach the table rather than the floor, where more than one frittata has landed in mid-flip.

Serves 8

2 tablespoons butter

1 cup chopped onion or leek (white and pale green parts only)

½ cup diced sweet red pepper

1 bunch thin asparagus, trimmed, cut on the diagonal into 1-inch pieces

1 cup sliced, stemmed shiitake mushrooms

1 cup freshly shelled peas

2 links chicken-apple sausage, sliced

3 ounces diced cream cheese or farmer's cheese

1 cup diced fontina or grated pecorino

16 eggs, beaten

1 teaspoon salt

Freshly ground pepper to taste

¼ cup freshly grated Parmesan

Preheat oven to 375°.

Melt the butter in a heavy 12-inch ovenproof skillet over medium heat. Add the onion or leek and sauté until translucent, 4–5 minutes. Add the remaining vegetables and sausage and sprinkle lightly with salt. Sauté until the vegetables are tender, another 5–6 minutes.

Whisk the eggs with 1 teaspoon of salt. Scatter the farmer's and fontina cheese over the vegetables in the skillet and pour the eggs on top. Stir gently to lift the vegetables into the egg mixture and grate some pepper over the eggs. Sprinkle the top with Parmesan. Let the eggs set slightly for 2–3 minutes and then place the skillet in the preheated oven.

Bake for 20 minutes at 375°, or until the top is lightly browned and slightly puffed. The traditional sign that it's done is that the edges and top are firm, but when you shake the pan the middle still jiggles slightly "like a young lady's belly" (apparently a lady without an Ab Machine or personal trainer).

Slice into wedges and serve with a green salad and potato strips.

CHEESES

Pecorino is a sheep's milk cheese with a sharp flavor and straw-white color. One of Italy's oldest cheeses, legend says a shepherd filled his leather flask with sheep's milk, and the motion of the long trip caused the milk to ferment. Much of the cheese is produced in Sardinia, although if you're lucky, you'll be able to get some from Bellwether Farms in California (see *Resources*).

Fontina is another ancient Italian cheese. Dense and slightly elastic, it is straw-colored with little round holes and good acidity. There's a delicate nuttiness to the taste, with a bit of earthiness like mushrooms, which makes it work well with the shiitake in this recipe, and gives it a taste of springtime when new life is breaking out of the earth. Fontina can also be served as a dessert cheese with fruit.

Parmesan is an unpasturized hard cheese made in Parma, Italy, from skimmed cow's milk, and has never come in a green cardboard can. It is created in 75-pound wheels with a very hard yellow rind. When cut, the inside is yellow and has a sweet and fruity aroma. The taste is quite piquant and occasionally slightly salty. Frequently grated over pasta, soups or salads, wafer-thin pieces can also be enjoyed as a dessert cheese. So valued is Parmesan that trucks delivering it to market have been hijacked at gunpoint.

Wine suggestion
Sangiovese

Potato strips

Somewhere between a chip and a fry, these potatoes are thin and crispy to add a bit of crunch when served with the fritatta and can be baked in the oven at the same time.

Serves 6–8

1 large, long russet potato

2 tablespoons vegetable oil

Preheat oven to 450°.

Slice the potato in long thin strips using a mandoline, if you have one, or a knife.

Soak the potato slices in cold water for 10 minutes to remove some of the excess starch. Dry them thoroughly and toss with the oil. Place the strips on a baking pan with raised edges. Salt liberally. Bake at 450° for 20–25 minutes, turning them occasionally, until they're crispy.

TRIPLE-THREAT CHOCOLATE ZUCCHINI MUFFINS

I found these flowerpots in a gourmet shop years ago, but any unglazed standard pot can be used. Just be sure to cover the hole in the bottom with a piece of aluminum foil. Even my husband, who avoids vegetables and claims he doesn't like anything green, wolfs down these muffins.

Makes 18 flowerpots or standard muffins

3 cups flour

⅓ cup cocoa powder

1 tablespoon baking powder

½ teaspoon baking soda

1½ teaspoons salt

2 teaspoons cinnamon

1 teaspoon freshly grated nutmeg

½ teaspoon ground cloves

½ cup milk

2 eggs, lightly beaten

¾ cup vegetable oil

1 cup sugar

2 cups shredded zucchini

1 cup chocolate chips

1 cup chocolate nibs or substitute chopped nuts (walnuts, pecans, macadamias…)

Preheat oven to 400°.

Mix dry ingredients together. Mix the milk, eggs, oil and sugar together and add to the dry ingredients. Add zucchini, chips and nibs and mix just until blended. Spoon the batter into greased pots or muffin tins and bake at 400° for 12–15 minutes until the top bounces back when tapped lightly with your finger.

"A little chocolate is like a love affair - an occasional sweet release that lightens the spirit. A lot of chocolate is like marriage - it seems so good at first but before you know it you've got chunky hips and a waddle-walk."

Linda Solegato

FRESH MELON WITH FRIZZLED PROSCIUTTO

Melon and prosciutto are a classic combination of sweet and juicy paired with salty and savory. By crisping the prosciutto in the oven, you add a crunchy note to the mix. Serve with blue cheese crackers (see *Pantry*, page 277) and an icy cold Truchard Albariño or Terraces Chardonnay for a sensuous start to a summer day.

2 melons of different colors, such as cantalope or charentais with honeydew

½ pound thinly sliced prosciutto

1 lime

1 tablespoon minced mint leaves

Choosing melons

Melons should be fragrant and yield slightly when you press a finger near the belly button. Cantalope will have a well-defined netting design etched on the skin when ripe. Honeydew should be smooth and feel very slightly dewy, not dry. The skins should be firm, without soft spots, and if you shake the melon, you should hear the seeds moving. Charentais are the most sensuous of melons. Deliciously musky, when sold in France they have a split in the side, which indicates ripeness. In the US, you have to grow them yourself or know a farmer to get a split one, but one that's intact will continue to ripen if left out of the refrigerator for a day or so.

Wine suggestions
Sauvignon Blanc; Muscadet; Syrah

TO PREPARE THE MELON AND SALSA

Slice the melon in half and remove the seeds and skin. Carve half of the melons into crescent shapes and one-quarter into chunks, and the rest into small dice.

Place the crescents and chunks in a bowl and squeeze the juice from ½ lime over the top. Refrigerate to keep the melon cool until serving time.

Place the diced melon in a bowl, drizzle with the juice from the remaining ½ lime, and toss with the mint leaves. Refrigerate until needed.

TO PREPARE THE PROSCIUTTO

Preheat oven to 375°.

Drape slices of the prosciutto on a cookie sheet in curly shapes. Or use an upside-down mini-muffin tin and curl the meat around the cups. Place in the oven for 5–10 minutes until the meat is crispy. Thicker slices take longer than thinly sliced prosciutto.

TO SERVE

Arrange melon slices and chunks on a plate with the crispy prosciutto. Garnish with the salsa and blue cheese crackers.

CHOCOLATE ZABAGLIONE

The definition of rich and sinfully delicious, the sweet tang of marsala plays off the bittersweet chocolate while the smoothness of the mixture spreads over every tastebud in your mouth. Serve it with perfect fresh raspberries or sliced white peaches. For a gently mocha version, grind the chocolate in your coffee grinder to pick up a subtle coffee taste.

Makes 1½ cups

8 egg yolks
½ cup sugar
¾ cup marsala wine
Pinch of salt

4 ounces semi-sweet chocolate, ground up in a food processor
1 cup whipped cream

Whisk the yolks, sugar, wine and salt in a heat-proof bowl – copper if you have it. Bring 1 or 2 inches of water to a boil in a medium-sized saucepan. Place the bowl over, but not touching, the boiling water and whisk constantly. The mixture will bubble up and then settle down after about 2 minutes. Keep whisking until the mixture thickens to the consistency of soft butter. Remove the bowl from the heat and add the chocolate. Whisk until the chocolate is melted in and the mixture cools. Fold in whipped cream. Can be refrigerated until serving time, but is best if not served icy cold.

"What you see before you, my friend, is the result of a lifetime of chocolate."
Katherine Hepburn

Chocolate For Everyone

CHOCOLATE HAZELNUT BISCOTTI

Biscotti are twice-baked cookies. Traditionally, the cookie dough is rolled into a log, baked, sliced and baked again. These biscotti are even easier as the dough is moist and can be patted into shape on the cookie sheet for the first baking. Often served in Italy with a *vin santo* or sweet dessert wine, or for breakfast with an espresso, and perhaps a shot of grappa, these cookies could also be dipped in melted chocolate or frosted on one side. As an alternative, soak dried cranberries or cherries in the same dessert wine you'll be serving, then drain and add to the batter.

Makes 5–6 dozen

1 cup sugar

½ cup melted butter (1 stick)

3 eggs

¼ teaspoon salt

1 tablespoon vanilla

1 cup chocolate nibs (or substitute chopped hazelnuts or walnuts or…)

2 cups chocolate chips

2 cups plus 2 tablespoons flour

1 tablespoon baking powder

⅓ cup cocoa powder

½ teaspoon freshly grated nutmeg

½ teaspoon cinnamon

¼ teaspoon freshly ground pepper

Equipment: A cookie sheet lined with a Silpat sheet or parchment paper.

Preheat oven to 350°.

Beat the sugar and butter in a mixing bowl. Add the eggs, salt and vanilla and continue mixing. Stir in the nibs and chips.

Put a sieve over a bowl and sift the remaining ingredients through it. Add them to the wet ingredients and use a wooden spoon or spatula to fold them together.

This is a moist and pliable dough. Divide it in half and form into 2 logs on a cookie sheet, each 15 inches long, 2–3 inches wide and an inch thick.

Bake for half an hour until they're firm when pressed with your finger. Put the cookie sheet on a cooling rack and let the logs reach room temperature. Don't try to cut them when they're warm or they'll crumble.

Slice the logs diagonally to create ½-inch or thinner cookies and place them on the same cookie sheet. Place the end pieces cut-side down. If you cut the cookies too thick, they'll be tough rather than crispy.

Bake for another 20–25 minutes until they're crisp and dry. Let them cool completely on the sheet before moving them to an airtight container.

HARRY'S GRILLED SALMON with ZUCCHINI CURRY SAUCE

This recipe for zucchini curry sauce was given to me 25 years ago by a sympathetic chef at Harry's Bar in Venice. We were dining with a charming gentleman from the Italian Embassy and as I swooned with delight at our dinner, he convinced the chef that sharing the recipe was the only way to revive me. Served here with grilled salmon, the original was poached in a flavorful court bouillon. I've also served the sauce with salmon ravioli, broiled sea scallops, and other firm, flavorful, sweet fish.

Salmon ingredients

Salmon filet
Butter or olive oil to keep it from sticking

Alternative: If you have a charcoal or gas grill, spread some olive oil on the salmon so that it doesn't stick and grill in the same fashion – flesh down to start, and then skin-side down to finish.

Harry's Bar zucchini curry sauce ingredients (makes 3 cups)

2 cups water
1½ pounds zucchini cut into 1-inch chunks (4 medium-small)
1 medium onion, sliced
2 tablespoons red wine vinegar
Freshly ground white pepper
⅛ teaspoon cayenne

2 tablespoons olive oil
1 celery rib, chopped
1 medium onion, chopped
3 tablespoons red wine vinegar
1 tablespoon butter
2 tablespoons flour
1 teaspoon curry powder
1 cup milk
½ teaspoon salt, or more to taste

TO PREPARE THE SALMON

Grill. OK, perhaps a little more information is called for, but it really is that simple.

Melt a tablespoon or two of butter in a skillet over medium-high heat. Place the salmon flesh down, skin-side up, in the bubbling butter.

Turn the heat down to medium and let the salmon cook for 5–7 minutes until it's crispy and browned on the outside, but still soft when you poke it – which means the inside is still rare. Flip the salmon over and cook for another 2–3 minutes until the inside is medium rare. Stick a knife in and peek if you're unsure. Serve with the zucchini sauce.

HARRY'S BAR ZUCCHINI CURRY SAUCE

Place the water in a saucepan and add the zucchini, sliced onion, 2 tablespoons of vinegar, white and red pepper and bring to a boil. Cover the pan, reduce the heat slightly, and simmer until the zucchini and onions are soft – 15 to 20 minutes.

Meanwhile… Heat olive oil in a small skillet over medium-low heat. Add the chopped celery and onion and cook until the vegetables are soft and golden – about 10 minutes. Add 3 tablespoons of vinegar and boil for 5 minutes. Stir in ½ cup of the liquid from the zucchini and boil for another couple of minutes. Add this mixture back to the zucchini.

Curry sauce *(continued)*

Purée in a food processor until smooth. Melt the butter in a large saucepan over medium heat. Add the flour and curry powder and whisk for a couple of minutes. Gradually whisk in the milk, then the zucchini mixture and blend completely. Boil over medium-high heat, for about 10 minutes until slightly thickened. Stir frequently. Season to taste and strain through a fine sieve.

Wine suggestion
Pinot Noir

Zucchini squash flower fritters

Anyone who's ever grown zucchini knows their secretive ways. No matter how often you pick them, somehow suddenly there's a motherlode of green baseball bats which apparently have been hiding under the leaves until they were ready to surprise you. One of the most delicious ways to combat this squash overproduction problem is to practice a little zucchini birth control by picking the flowers.

Each plant will have both boy and girl flowers. The boys have a long slim stem joining the flower to the plant and the petals tend to be wide open – little squash flashers that they are. The girls will have a baby zucchini at the base and the petals are closed and coy. Both make delicious fritters.

12–16 zucchini flowers, including any baby squashes that are attached (or you can use day lilies or large nasturtium)

¾ cup flour

1 cup water

1 teaspoon salt

Optional: a small handful of fresh, finely chopped herbs (thyme, parsley, oregano...)

Oil for deep frying

Clean the zucchini flowers gently. Trim the stems. Blend the water, flour and salt to a smooth batter. Mix in the herbs.

Heat 2 inches of oil in a deep frying pan to 350° (a drop of the batter will sizzle and dance on the surface). Dip the flowers into the batter and then gently slide into the oil. Turn when golden brown. Remove and drain on a kitchen towel. Sprinkle with salt and pepper and serve hot.

Optional: These fritters are also wonderful stuffed. Blend together 6–8 ounces fresh goat cheese, a crushed clove of garlic, a pinch of fresh thyme, one beaten egg, salt and freshly ground pepper and a dash of milk to soften the mixture. Spoon carefully into the flowers, making sure the petals completely enclose the mixture. Then dip the flowers in the batter and proceed as instructed above.

Spanish Exploration

That's Maya piece of chocolate!

Eggs de Seville

Chocolate flan torta

Garlic soup

Fresh from the farm

Hot chocolate for grown-ups

Figs five ways

Tortilla Española

eggs de Seville

CHOCOLATE FLAN TORTA

While a can opener doesn't get much play in our kitchen, we make an exception for this recipe in the name of authenticity – and the fact that it's a dense chocolately caramel taste bomb. When our helpers take turns saying "she did it" in response to "who ate all of the chocolate flan?" I know we've got a winner. The texture is somewhere between a cake and a traditional flan.

Serves 8

Chocolate batter ingredients

¾ cup dulce de leche (see page 36 or purchased)
1 cup sugar
¾ cup flour
½ cup cocoa powder
¾ teaspoon salt
¾ teaspoon baking powder
¾ teaspoon baking soda

¼ cup oil
½ cup milk
1 teaspoon vanilla
1 egg

½ cup boiling water

Flan batter ingredients

6 ounces cream cheese
5 eggs
¾ cup evaporated milk – goat's milk if available
1 can of sweetened condensed milk

TO PREPARE

Preheat oven to 350°.

Divide the dulce de leche among eight 1-cup buttered ramekins, spreading it evenly with a rubber spatula.

The chocolate batter: Place the dry ingredients in a mixing bowl. Mix in everything else except the boiling water. When the batter is well incorporated, add the boiling water. Ladle the batter over the dulce in each ramekin.

The flan: Mix the cream cheese, eggs and a splash of the milk to loosen the cheese. Add the remaining milks and blend well. Pour the flan over the chocolate batter in each ramekin.

TO BAKE

Place the ramekins in a baking pan and add hot water to reach halfway up the sides of the ramekins. Bake at 350° for 45 minutes until a toothpick stuck in the center comes out clean. Remove the ramekins from the water and let them cool.

TO SERVE

Run a knife around the edge of the torta to loosen it from the ramekin. Firmly hold a plate over the ramekin and turn it upside down. Give it a little shake if necessary. To gild the lily, serve the torta with a scoop of vanilla or cinnamon ice cream and sliced peaches that have soaked in Champagne or a Spanish cava.

Wine suggestions
Spanish cava or California sparkling wine from one of the Spanish houses, Artesa or Gloria Ferrar

GARLIC SOUP

With eggs and toast, it must be breakfast, but if you'd like to prepare this as a first course instead of the main meal, use only one slice of bread and one egg per person.

Serves 2 for breakfast/brunch
or 4 as a starter

2 tablespoons olive oil

3 cloves garlic

4 slices sour-dough baguette or other country-style bread, cut ½-inch thick

2 teaspoons paprika

½ teaspoon cumin seeds, crushed

3+ cups hearty beef or veal stock

Dash of cayenne

Salt to taste

4 eggs

2 tablespoons freshly chopped parsley

Wine suggestion
Tempranillo

Heat olive oil in a medium saucepan over medium-high heat. Drop the garlic cloves in and sauté them, stirring frequently. They'll puff and turn golden brown and soft. Remove and set aside.

Brown the bread slices on both sides in the olive oil in the pan.

Let the pan cool off a little and add the paprika and cumin, which will absorb the rest of the oil. Then add the beef stock and the garlic cloves, which you've crushed with a fork. Stir well. Taste and add salt if needed. Simmer the soup for about 10 minutes.

Place 2 slices browned bread in each bowl. Poach the eggs in the soup by cracking each egg into a small bowl and slipping it off into the simmering broth. Leave it there until the white firms up but the yolk is still soft – about 4 minutes. Remove each egg with a slotted spoon and place it on a slice of bread. Spoon the soup over the top and sprinkle with fresh minced parsley.

HOT CHOCOLATE for GROWN-UPS

When Spanish explorers brought chocolate home from the Americas, it was adopted with such enthusiasm that the Pope had to intervene to request that ladies refrain from drinking hot chocolate in church. As the story goes, the custom was so popular that he was unsuccessful in his appeal. Ah, to relive those decadent times.

Serves 4

1 vanilla bean

4 cups whole milk

½ cup cream (optional)

5 ounces of bittersweet chocolate, broken into pieces

2 tablespoons sugar

¼ cup cognac or brandy

Whipped cream

A sprinkling of cocoa powder

Split the vanilla bean lengthwise with the tip of a sharp knife and scrape out the seeds. Add the seeds and the bean to the milk and cream in a saucepan. Bring the mixture almost to a boil and turn off the heat to let the vanilla infuse the milk for 5 minutes or longer, and then remove the bean.

In a separate saucepan, melt the chocolate in a little of the hot milk. Stir the melted chocolate into the remaining hot vanilla/milk with the sugar. Ladle the hot chocolate into a beautiful cup or small brandy snifter. Pour the cognac on top and add the whipped cream and a sprinkling of cocoa powder.

FIGS FIVE WAYS

To my great disappointment, our first California home had three varieties of fig trees rather than the citrus grove I'd imagined. My only prior experience with figs involved removing seeds from between my teeth after trying a Fig Newton cookie. Then I tasted a fresh fig. Miraculous. Fresh off the tree, warm from the sun, dodging the bees who love them as well… sweet, but never cloying, luscious without dripping, delicate, fragrant and beautifully shaped, figs might just be the most sensual fruit. And the trees provide all of those fig leaves for party favors. And we know what trouble that created.

Delicious fresh figs pair with creamy mascarpone or salty prosciutto. Transformed by heat, which coaxes the delicate flavor out of fresh figs, they turn jammy and mingle beautifully with blue cheese, balsamic vinegar and, of course, chocolate. At their mushy ripest, when there's a honey-like drop of moisture on the skin and they're about 15 minutes away from bursting, figs are at their most delicious. To capture this moment, create a fresh fig sorbet, adding nothing more than a little sugar and lemon juice.

Five ways aren't enough, but it's a start.

Serves 6

6 figs
½ cup mascarpone cheese

Fig chutney ingredients

2 tablespoons minced shallot
¼ cup balsamic vinegar
1 teaspoon freshly grated ginger
6 fresh figs, minced
A sprinkling of sea salt

FRESH FIGS

Gently clean each fig and cut off the stem. Pull it apart in four directions from the top, leaving the bulbous bottom intact. (Or cut it in quarters almost to the bottom if you find that easier.) Fill it with a generous spoonful of mascarpone cheese, and serve topped with fresh fig sorbet (see *Frozen Delights*, page 261).

FIG CHUTNEY

Place the shallot, balsamic and ginger in a small saucepan over medium-high heat until the vinegar is reduced by half. Remove the pan from the heat and toss in the figs to let them absorb the liquid and cook slightly in it. Sprinkle a small pinch of sea salt over the top and set the mixture aside for half an hour, or store it in the refrigerator until you're ready to serve it.

Grilled fig ingredients

6 fresh figs, stems discarded and halved lengthwise

¼ cup fresh Gorgonzola or other blue cheese

Roasted fig ingredients

6 fresh figs

6 pieces of semi-sweet chocolate – use either broken bits of half of a 7-ounce semi-sweet bar, or 4–5 chocolate chips per fig

Fig varieties

History places figs (and, more importantly, their leaves) in the garden of Eden, with the ancient pharaohs in Egypt, and then in Crete and Greece, where they were so esteemed that laws forbade their export. Thousands of years have led to a wide range of color and subtlety in texture, with reportedly over 150 different varieties. Some of the more readily available are:

- **Black mission:** blackish-purple skin and pink flesh, intense flavor
- **Calimyrna:** greenish-yellow skin and amber flesh, delicate texture
- **Brown Turkey:** purple skin and red flesh, often found in California home gardens
- **Kadota:** green skin and purplish flesh

Wine suggestion
Demi-sec sparkling wine

GRILLED FIGS WITH GORGONZOLA

Preheat the broiler and place the rack 6 inches below the heat source. In most ovens this position is the one below the top spot.

Place the fig halves cut-side up in the middle of a baking sheet. Place one teaspoon of cheese on each half. Broil until the cheese melts and bubbles – generally 3–4 minutes. Either serve immediately or turn off the broiler and move the baking sheet to a lower shelf to keep warm until you're ready to serve.

CHOCOLATE-STUFFED AND ROASTED FIGS

Preheat oven to 375°.

With a sharp paring knife, cut a slit in the bottom of each fig. Stuff it with a piece of chocolate. Place the fig on its side on a baking sheet and roast for 10 minutes until the chocolate is melted and runny.

Alternatively, if you're making the grilled figs, place these chocolate-stuffed figs on the outside edge of the baking sheet when it goes under the broiler. These stuffed figs won't be under direct heat, but will receive enough reflected warmth to melt the chocolate. Serve warm.

FIVE MORE ALTERNATIVES

Serve fresh fig halves wrapped in prosciutto, or if they're under-ripe, poach them in red wine with a vanilla bean and a shake of cinnamon and serve drizzled with honey. Slice them on a pizza with blue cheese, using the pizza recipe on page 66. Add sliced figs to a lightly dressed salad of arugula, fresh Parmesan shavings and freshly ground black pepper. Stuff fresh figs with goat cheese and sprinkle chopped pine nuts on top.

TORTILLA ESPAÑOLA

This is a specialty of Shirlee Quick, my kitchen kindred spirit, staff Spanish translator and cooking co-conspirator. To our benefit, she learned this most traditional of Spanish dishes from "Las Señoras" while she was a graduate student in Barcelona.

Serves 6 to 8 as a main course or makes 40+ appetizers

6 or 7 large red potatoes, sliced ⅛-inch thick on a mandoline or by hand (feel free to leave the skins on or you can peel them) – should yield 5 cups cooked

1 large yellow onion, sliced thinly in half moons

Olive oil – about ½ cup by the time you're done

Salt and freshly ground pepper to taste (don't be afraid to use a fair amount of salt – the potatoes can take it)

5 large eggs (if the eggs are on the smallish side, add another one)

Garnish (parsley or other peppery green salad)

Preheat oven to 375°.

Combine sliced potatoes and onions in a large bowl and generously salt and pepper them (a touch of olive oil will prevent browning while you do this). Make sure all of the potato mixture gets salt. Taste a raw piece to make sure.

In a large pan with a lid, heat several tablespoons of olive oil. Add potatoes and stir to coat with oil. Cook uncovered for a few minutes then turn heat to low, cover with a tight-fitting lid and let them steam and cook for about 15–20 minutes. Potatoes should be tender but hold their shape, though a few will disintegrate. And yes, there will be some very brown crust on the bottom of the pan. It's okay – it will clean with a bit of soaking.

Pour potato mixture from the pan into a colander or strainer to drain off the excess oil. The mixture can be refrigerated at this point or used immediately.

Beat eggs in a large bowl until well combined. Lightly season with salt and pepper. Pour the potato mixture into the eggs and, using your hands, combine the eggs and potatoes until the potatoes are well coated with egg and there's only loose egg around the edges.

Heat 3 tablespoons of olive oil in a 9-inch heavy skillet (I prefer All-Clad) until almost smoking. Pour the potato mixture in all at once and use a spatula to evenly distribute the potatoes. Keep shaking the pan to ensure that the omelet is loose and not sticking to the pan. Put it in the oven to finish cooking – 20 minutes or so. The center should be firm but not dry. (The traditional method is to slide the omelet onto a plate and then invert back into the pan to finish cooking. The oven is much easier.)

Once out of the oven, cover the skillet with a large plate, and grasping the plate and skillet firmly together, invert them and turn omelet out onto the plate. BE CAREFUL – THE PAN IS HOT AND ANY EXTRA OIL MAY DRIP ONTO YOUR HAND.

Garnish with a parsley salad dressed with your favorite extra virgin olive oil and lemon. Grate Parmesan generously over the salad and toss again. Taste for seasoning.

Cut the tortilla into wedges as a main course or into squares for appetizers. Serve warm or at room temperature.

Note: *Romesco sauce (see Pantry, page 273) or any green, parsley based sauce would be good with this.*

Wine suggestions
Tempranilla; Albarino

Ode to a
Chocolate Truffle

a chocolatey poem by tony

I see you sitting there, you minx,
With my seatmate to the right,
A lovely dark chocolate truffle,
Given to each passenger on our flight.

Yes, I devoured your cousin,
Seconds whence he hit my plate,
But you, you darling chocolate treat,
You've dodged his gruesome fate.

And now 2B is sleeping,
And he's left you, his sweet, untouched,
You're sitting there…you call to me!
God! I love you oh so much!

They say you're a luxury,
Something to savor. Something rare.
But for me you are the stuff of life,
And you're just sitting there!

In seconds I could reach across,
And grab you from his tray
2B wouldn't notice…would he?
If I carried you away…

I would devour your chocolate skin
And your coco heart divine,
I want you 2B's truffle,
I want to make you mine!

What's this? 2B is stirring!
Waking from his fitful sleep!
He's reaching for HIS truffle,
And to action I must leap!

But he's too quick and grabs you
Clothed in your paper shroud
"Are you going to eat that truffle?"
I hear myself scream loud!

"Why no," he says responding,
"Would you like it for yourself?"
Like a man possessed I grab you,
And in my mouth you melt.

Where once there was a man obsessed
With chocolate smooth and creamy,
Now there exists a man sublime,
Oh truffle…you were dreamy!

The French Connection

Liberté, Egalité, Chocolaté

Chocolate croissant meets French toast

Baked pears over vanilla cognac sauce

Chocolate-filled toast pillows

Comme les Americains

Chocolate banana strudel

Baked eggs

Orange muffins

Champagne to start

Mimosa sunrise

Chocolate strawberry dumpling

Camembert cheese pancake

Squash sweet and savory

Steamed pumpkin pudding

Butternut squash ravioli with black walnut brown-butter sauce

Gougère – cheese puffs

*chocolate croissant
meets French toast*

BAKED PEARS over VANILLA COGNAC SAUCE

My favorite 'comment' on this dish came from Michael James Holloway, one of our favorite guests who was here with his parents, Anne and Jack. With the joyous lack of inhibitions of a four-year-old, after finishing the pear he turned the bowl upside down and licked the last remnants of sauce to make sure none got away.

Pear ingredients

3 ripe pears
½ cup raisins
2 tablespoons cognac or brandy
¼ cup sugar
2 tablespoons butter
2 teaspoons cinnamon
½ teaspoon freshly grated nutmeg

Vanilla sauce ingredients

1½ cups cream or half-and-half
**1½ teaspoons vanilla extract
  (or use a whole vanilla bean)**
1 tablespoon cognac or brandy
3 tablespoons sugar
2 egg yolks

Finishing ingredients

**6 mini scoops of pear-Champagne
  sorbet (see *Frozen Delights*,
  page 262), or blend 2 tablespoons
  of pear liqueur into ½ cup vanilla
  ice cream**
6 mint sprigs

TO PREPARE THE PEARS

Preheat oven to 375°.

Peel each pear and cut it in half, starting at the stem end. Cut out the core, leaving the stem intact on one of the halves if possible for presentation. Cut a thin slice off the rounded back so the pear sits flat on the plate. Rub the pear with lemon juice so it won't turn brown.

Blend the remaining ingredients in a food processor or blender until finely mixed.

Fill the hollowed core of each pear half with a heaped portion of the raisin-cognac mixture. Place pears close together in a buttered baking dish and cover the dish loosely with foil. Bake for 25 minutes at 375°.

TO MAKE THE VANILLA SAUCE

Mix cream, vanilla, cognac and sugar in a medium saucepan. Heat just to a boil as tiny bubbles begin to show around the edge. Turn the heat to low while you whisk the egg yolks in a small bowl. Continue to whisk the yolks as you add one tablespoon of the hot cream mixture at a time until the yolks are warmed. Add the warmed yolks to the cream mixture in the pan.

Make the raisin/cognac filling and refrigerate it in a closed container. It might actually taste even better the next day, as this gives the flavors more time to blend.

Stir the mixture with a wooden spoon until the sauce thickens enough to coat the back of the spoon. (Don't let it boil or you'll have vanilla-flavored scrambled eggs.)

TO SERVE

Arrange each warm pear half on a pool of vanilla sauce and garnish with a mint sprig at the stem end. A dollop of icy cold pear-Champagne sorbet on top of the warm pear completes the dish.

CHOOSING PEARS

When purchasing pears, check for ripeness by pressing the stem end lightly. If it yields, the pear is ready to eat. If you have hard pears, place them in a paper bag to ripen for a few days. Three varieties that are good choices for baking are:

Anjou or d'Anjou: With a mild flavor and juicy texture, Anjous are firm enough to hold up to baking. Yellowish-green and occasionally red, they have thin skins that turn more yellow as they ripen. They last longer at the ripe stage than Bartletts or Bosc, so if you're shopping ahead of time, get Anjou.

Bartlett: Very aromatic and the most flavorful, but ripe Bartletts hit their peak for only a day or two, then turn to mush. They are sometimes red but generally green, turning to yellow as they ripen.

Bosc: Flavorful and firm-fleshed, Boscs bake well. Their brown skins don't change color upon ripening, and they have a long neck that can be tricky to keep intact.

USING A VANILLA BEAN

Using a vanilla bean instead of vanilla extract will give you a rich, intense vanilla flavor, plus the beauty of the little seeds floating in the sauce. Beans are available at gourmet shops where spices are sold, and from spice suppliers like Penzey's or Whole Spice. See *Resources* for contact information.

Starting at one end and running down the length of the bean, use the point of a knife to cut halfway though the bean, exposing the seeds on the inside. (Don't worry if you cut all the way through here and there. It will still work just fine.) Scrape out the seeds with the edge of the knife blade and add them and the scraped bean to the cream instead of the vanilla extract. After the mixture reaches a boil, turn off the heat and let the vanilla steep for 15 minutes before continuing with the egg yolks. Remove the bean before serving the sauce.

If you're really planning ahead, you can soak the bean in the cognac, which will make both taste wonderful and will soften the bean, making it even easier to cut. Chef Gary Danko keeps his vanilla beans in a tall pasta jar topped up with cognac. They're soft enough that you can just cut off the end and squeeze the seeds out like a tube of toothpaste.

"Put 'eat chocolate' at the top of your list of things to do today. That way, at least you'll get one thing done."

CHOCOLATE-FILLED TOAST PILLOWS

Most people guess these are beignets rather than pieces of French bread stuffed with chocolate and dipped in a batter. But this is a miracle batter. It's thick enough to coat easily, yet liquid enough to soften whatever is dipped into it. I think you could dip your left shoe in it and the result would be tender.

As alternatives to the chocolate-filled bread, try peanut butter stuffed dates or use dried apple rings. Sprinkle them with cinnamon sugar rather than powdered sugar and they look and taste like little apple doughnuts.

Batter ingredients

2 cups flour
½ cup sugar
4 teaspoons baking powder
½ teaspoon ground cinnamon
½ teaspoon freshly grated nutmeg
½ teaspoon salt
1 teaspoon vanilla
1 egg, lightly beaten
1¾ cups milk
2 teaspoons vegetable or canola oil

Toast pillow ingredients

1 baguette (18–24-inch long French bread)
2 bittersweet or dark chocolate bars broken into 1-inch square pieces (1.5 ounces)
Vegetable or canola oil for deep-frying

Night owl instructions

Slice the bread and fill the pockets with chocolate. Keep at room temperature overnight in a plastic bag or airtight container.

TO PREPARE THE BATTER

Mix all of the dry ingredients together in a mixing bowl. Add the rest of the ingredients and beat until the batter is smooth.

TO PREPARE THE TOAST PILLOWS

Cut the baguette into ¾-inch-thick slices. Cut a pocket in each slice by inserting a sharp paring knife through the crust at the top of the piece of bread. Wiggle the knife back and forth so that the pocket inside is bigger than the hole. Put a piece of chocolate in the pocket. Allow 2–3 slices per person.

Hint: If the bread is very soft and you're having trouble stuffing it, throw it in the freezer for 20 minutes or so and it will harden enough to handle.

Heat 2 inches of oil in a deep frying pan over medium-high heat until it reaches 350° on a deep-fry thermometer.

Place a piece of paper towel over several layers of newspaper on a baking sheet. This is where you'll put the cooked pillows so the paper can absorb any excess oil.

Preheat oven to 200°.

117

Ingredients to assemble

4–5 tablespoons lemon curd (available at grocers and gourmet shops ready-made, or make it yourself with the recipe in the *Pantry*, page 277)

1 cup Vermont or other real maple syrup (preferably grade B as it's the most flavorful)

2 tablespoons Cointreau or other orange liqueur (optional)

2–3 tablespoons powdered (confectioner's) sugar

1 lemon and 1 lime for zest (or use an orange)

Citrus zest curls

Zest is the skin of citrus fruit without the bitter white pith that's just beneath the skin. Citrus zesters are available at kitchen supply stores and make it easy to create curls by just dragging the tool across the skin. Lacking a zester, you can peel the zest off the fruit with a sharp paring knife (being careful to leave the white pith behind) and then slice the zest into fine, long strips.

Testing hot oil without a thermometer

If you don't have a thermometer, heat the oil until your hand feels hot when you hold it 4 inches over the pan. Then test the temperature by dipping a small piece of bread in the batter and dropping it into the hot oil. If it sinks, the oil isn't hot enough. It should puff up and get lightly brown in a minute or two. If it gets dark brown in less than a minute, turn the heat down.

Using tongs, pick up a chocolate-filled slice of bread and dip it in the batter. Let any excess batter drip off, and then gently place the coated bread in the hot oil. It should come right to the top and start to puff. In a minute or two, when the edges get golden brown, turn it over and cook the other side. Remove to the absorbent paper. Spread lemon curd gently over the pillow as though you were buttering toast. The heat from the pillow will make it melt and spread easily.

Depending on the size of your pan, you can probably cook six pillows at a time. As each batch is done, leave them on the baking sheet and put the whole thing in the oven to keep warm while you prepare the rest.

TO ASSEMBLE

Combine maple syrup and Cointreau in a small saucepan and warm over medium heat. For each person, arrange 3 toast pillows on a plate in a semicircle.

Place the powdered sugar in a sifter or a shaker. Dust the toast with the powdered sugar. Top with curls of lemon and lime zest to create a delicious aroma and a hint of what's ahead. Pass around warmed maple/orange syrup in a pitcher.

Wine suggestions
The vanilla flavors in an oak-aged Chardonnay mirror the flavors of the baked pears and vanilla sauce, and the citrus aromas found in some Chardonnay complement the lemon in the toast pillows. Avoid particularly buttery Chardonnay for this menu. One with higher acid will stand up better to the richness of the vanilla sauce, as would Blanc de Blanc or sparkling wine made from Chardonnay.

CHOCOLATE BANANA STRUDEL

Strudel ingredients

2 tablespoons butter for the bananas

4 bananas, peeled and split lengthwise

8 sheets filo dough

¼ cup melted butter for the filo

¼ cup brown sugar

½ cup chocolate chips

Caramel sauce ingredients

2 tablespoons butter

½ cup brown sugar

1 tablespoon cognac

TO MAKE THE STRUDEL

Preheat oven to 400°.

Melt the butter in a skillet over medium heat and gently add the bananas. When the bottom of the banana is golden brown, turn it over and cook the other side.

Place a sheet of filo on your work surface. Brush it with melted butter and top with another sheet. Top that with butter and fold it in half. You shoud have a 4-layered piece measuring 6 x 8 inches.

Put two halves of grilled banana near the 6-inch edge. Sprinkle with a tablespoon of brown sugar and 2 tablespoons of chocolate chips. Roll the bananas in the filo, then tuck in the edges and continue rolling. Place the package seam side down on a greased cookie sheet. Continue with the other three. Brush all four packages with more melted butter.

Bake for 12–14 minutes until they turn golden brown.

TO MAKE THE CARAMEL SAUCE

Melt the butter in a small skillet over medium heat. Add the brown sugar and cognac and stir until they're combined and bubbling.

TO ASSEMBLE

Place a swirl of caramel sauce on each plate. Make a diagonal cut through the middle of each strudel. Place one half on the caramel sauce and balance the other half on top so that the luscious chocolately banana filling is visible.

BAKED EGGS

One of the most frequently requested breakfasts among returning guests, these eggs are probably the easiest to make, so we save it for the days when Vikki Rugg makes breakfast. When she first started working at the Inn, she was terrified that we'd make her cook. Apparently as a young bride she made her husband an offer that was too good to refuse. She told him he could choose one room in the house where she'd be very, very good. He didn't pick the kitchen.

Per serving

1 tablespoon cream
2 eggs
A pinch each of thyme, oregano and paprika
A dash of salt and a few grindings of pepper
3–4 tablespoons of grated cheese – a combination of cheddar, Swiss and Parmesan

Butter as many 8-ounce ramekins as you have hungry people to feed. Add a splash of cream and break two eggs into each ramekin. Sprinkle with the herbs and season with a pinch of salt and freshly ground pepper. Sprinkle cheese over the top.

Bake in a bain marie. (Put the ramekins in a pan and fill that pan with warm water half way up the sides of the ramekins. Four ramekins fit perfectly in a 9-inch square brownie pan.) Bake for 20–25 minutes at 375° until the cheese starts to puff up in the middle and brown lightly. Peek under the cheese by pulling it up with the tip of a knife. The whites should be completely set and the yolks beginning to thicken. Place the ramekins under a broiler for 60 seconds until the cheese sizzles and puffs up slightly. Serve immediately.

Hint: My favorite tool for removing hot ramekins from a bain marie, without poaching my fingers, is a jar lifter, which can be found wherever canning supplies are sold.

Alternatives: Sauté shiitake or portabello mushrooms, or broccoli, or julienned ham, or whatever else strikes your fancy and place it in the bottom of the ramekin before breaking eggs into it. Or criss-cross sautéed asparagus over the top before sprinkling with blue cheese. This is one of those recipes where you can vary the contents by what's fresh in the garden, or just keep it simple.

If you have extra egg whites available, add one to each ramekin. It will make the dish rise dramatically in the oven.

ORANGE MUFFINS

Makes 12–18 muffins

Muffin ingredients

1½ cups sugar

¾ cup butter, softened

3 eggs

2 tablespoons grated orange peel

½ cup fresh orange juice

2 teaspoons baking powder

½ teaspoon salt

2½ cups flour

Glaze ingredients

¼ cup fresh orange juice

½ cup powdered (confectioner's) sugar

Wine suggestion
Muscat

Heat oven to 400°. Grease a muffin pan or line it with paper cups.

In a large bowl, beat the sugar and butter together until light and fluffy. Add the eggs, one at a time, beating after each addition. The mixture will turn a fluffy pale yellow. Add the orange peel, juice and eggs; blend well. Add the baking powder and salt and blend again. Stir in the flour just until moistened.

Spoon the batter into each muffin cup, filling it ⅔ full. Place the pan in the middle of the oven and bake for 20 minutes, just until golden. Lightly tap the top of a muffin. If it holds your fingerprint, it's not done. If it bounces back, remove the pan from the oven.

Make a glaze by mixing the orange juice and powdered sugar. Brush it over the tops of the still-warm muffins and serve.

MIMOSA SUNRISE

Start the day with a glass of liquid sunshine, guaranteed to raise a smile and your spirits.

1 part orange juice

2 parts chilled Champagne or
    sparkling wine

¼ teaspoon of grenadine per glass

Fill a Champagne flute first with ⅓ orange juice and then ⅔ Champagne. Slowly drop grenadine in the glass and it will settle to the bottom, creating the sunrise. Serve with the proper ceremony.

When to drink Champagne

I drink it when I am happy, and when I am sad.
Sometimes I drink it when I am alone.
When I have company, I consider it obligatory.
I trifle with it if I am not hungry, and drink it when I am.
Otherwise I never touch it – unless I am thirsty.

Mme. Lilly Bollinger

CHOCOLATE STRAWBERRY DUMPLING

This is the dough for the timid. The cream cheese makes it so forgiving and easy to work with that if you make a hole in it when covering the strawberries, just slap some more dough on top and voila – all better. The dough can be made ahead and refrigerated for 2–3 days, or frozen for up to 3 weeks. If you only want to make a few dumplings, freeze the rest of the dough and use it to bake a tart crust to fill with fresh berries or peaches and whipped cream for a spectacular last-minute dessert.

Makes 12 big guys

Cream cheese pastry ingredients

2½ cups flour

½ cup cocoa powder

1 tablespoon sugar

2 teaspoons finely grated lemon zest

⅛ teaspoon salt

1½ sticks butter – 12 ounces – chilled and cut into ¼-inch slices

8 ounces cream cheese, cubed

12 perfect, very large, firm, very red strawberries, without white shoulders

12 mint sprigs

Vanilla ice cream or whipped cream

TO MAKE THE PASTRY

Place flour, cocoa, sugar, lemon zest and salt in a food processor and process for a few seconds (or mix in a bowl, using a fork). Then add the butter and pulse on and off until the mixture has a cornmeal consistency. Next, scatter the cream cheese over the mixture and process until the dough comes together in a ball. Flatten the dough into a 12 x 9-inch rectangle and wrap in plastic. Place in the refrigerator to chill for at least 3–4 hours.

Preheat the oven to 400° and put a rack in the lower half. Take the dough out of the refrigerator about 10 minutes before you need it, which gives you time to clean the strawberries in cold water, letting them dry on a towel. Pull off any leaves, but don't cut the berry as it will ooze a lot more juice when baking if the skin is broken.

TO MAKE THE DUMPLINGS

Cut the dough into 12 squares measuring 3 x 3 inches and place on a square of plastic wrap. Cover with another piece of wrap and roll out each piece of dough until it measures 5 square inches. Remove the plastic wrap and place the point of the bottom of the strawberry in the middle of the dough. Bring the opposite corners together over the berry to form a package, pressing the dough together to seal at the top and remove any air. With a toothpick, prick a few holes through the dough around the top to let steam escape.

Optional: To simulate the texture of the outside of a strawberry, roll the dumpling gently over the small holes on a grater – the ones you'd use to grate citrus peel or Parmesan. It looks just like a strawberry skin.

TO BAKE

Place the dumplings on a cookie sheet and bake at 400° for 30–35 minutes until they smell chocolately and the berries are steaming and oozing a bit of juice.

TO SERVE

They can be served warm or cold. Stick a mint sprig into the top of the dumpling where the leaves had been and serve with vanilla ice cream or a dollop of whipped cream.

Stone fruit alternatives: Use nectarines or peaches that are on the small side. The white ones are an especially delicious pairing with chocolate. Submerge peaches for 5 seconds in nearly boiling water first to remove the fuzz. Apricots are also a tasty contrast to the crunchy chocolate coating. There will be enough dough for 9 peaches or nectarines or a dozen apricots. When using any of these stone fruit, cut them in half around the equator, twist the halves in opposite directions and remove the pits. Replace the pit with filling, put the halves together again, and proceed in the same way as with the strawberries. As the fruit is larger, it'll probably need to cook for about 5 minutes more. When you think they're done, stick a fork in at the top of the peach or nectarine. It should go in easily with little resistance from the fruit.

Stone fruit filling ingredients

Mix together all of the following:

1 egg white

¼ cup sugar

¼ cup chocolate nibs (or toasted almonds, ground)

¼ cup Graham cracker crumbs

½ teaspoon vanilla (or almond) extract

⅛ teaspoon fine lemon zest

Camembert pancake, sweet version with strawberries

CAMEMBERT CHEESE PANCAKE

Encourage your guests to be seated and ready to eat, as once the pancakes come out of the oven, they'll deflate if they can't be served right away. They're still tasty, but the drama is gone.

Serves 8

½ cup butter

1½ cups flour

6 ounces of Camembert, soft Gorgonzola, Brie, or other bloomed-rind cheese , thinly sliced, with any hard bits of rind removed

6 eggs

1½ cups milk

½ teaspoon salt

Light sprinkling of cayenne pepper

1 cup minced chives

Wine suggestions
Barbera; Grenache

Preheat oven to 425°.

Divide butter among 8 low-sided ramekins and place them on cookie sheets (for ease in handling) in the very hot oven for 4–5 minutes. Remove when the butter is bubbling and not yet brown.

Meanwhile, mix the cheese and flour in a blender or food processor so the soft cheese breaks up before you add the milk, eggs and salt and mix briefly again.

Pour this egg batter into the hot melted butter in the ramekins, sprinkle with cayenne and place immediately in the oven. Bake for 20–25 minutes until the sides of the pancakes rise above the dishes and the edges become crisp and light brown. (Try to resist the temptation to peek earlier than 20 minutes or you risk having them flatten.) Serve immediately garnished with chives.

Alternative: *For a sweet version of this savory dish, omit the cayenne and chives and sprinkle the baked pancake with nutmeg and powdered sugar. Serve with sautéed pears, apples or peaches sprinkled with cinnamon and freshly grated nutmeg, strawberries or other fresh fruit or a fresh fruit jam or apple sauce.*

STEAMED PUMPKIN PUDDING

Lynn Brown of Forni-Brown Gardens was among the first to grow vegetables for local restaurant chefs, which means things are grown for flavor, not transport. He's the source for plants and seeds for our garden, as well as aid when there's a horticultural mystery. Lynn presented me with a magnificent tawny-colored Fairy Queen pumpkin to use in this pudding. If only you could taste the page.

Serves 8

1 stick unsalted butter, melted
    (½ cup)

1 cup sugar

1 cup puréed pumpkin pulp,
    homemade or canned

1 large egg

1 teaspoon vanilla

1 teaspoon cinnamon

½ teaspoon freshly grated nutmeg

1 teaspoon baking powder

1 teaspoon baking soda

1 teaspoon salt

½ cup whole milk

1 cup Heath bar chocolate toffee
    bits (or substitute mini chocolate
    chips)

1 cup flour

Special equipment: A lidded pudding mold or a deep two-quart bowl, plus a pot that will hold the mold or bowl comfortably.

I use a food processor to make this because it does a good job of puréeing the pumpkin, but you can also use a plain mixer or even a wooden spoon.

TO MAKE THE BATTER

Melt the butter. If you're using a pudding mold, pour the butter in and turn the mold around to make sure all of the nooks and crannies are coated. Pour the remainder of the melted butter into your mixer or food processor.

Add all of the other ingredients except the flour and mix them together thoroughly. Then add the flour and stir just until blended.

Pour the batter into the buttered mold or bowl and cover it. If using a bowl, cover it with buttered aluminum foil.

TO STEAM THE PUDDING

Fill a large pot with 3 inches of water and bring it to a simmer. Place a small plate or rack on the bottom of the pot to keep the mold from sitting directly on the pan.

Carefully place the mold in the simmering water, which should come about halfway up the side of the mold. Let it simmer away for an hour and a half. When it's done, remove the mold from the water bath and take off the lid. Put a serving plate over the mold and turn it upside down and then remove the mold.

Only in season for a month or two, persimmon is a delicious substitute for the pumpkin, and doesn't have to be cooked first.

There are two types of persimmon available here in California: Fuyu, which have a flat bottom, and Hachiya, which are heart-shaped with a pointed bottom. The Fuyu are ready to eat like an apple when the skin yields to slight pressure. Hachiya, on the other hand, are mouth-puckeringly astringent until they've either been through a freeze (on the tree or in your freezer) or have ripened until they are very soft. We have a wonderful source of Fuyu, so that's what I use, but Hachiya also work beautifully. If you use Fuyu, peel and core them and then purée. With Hachiya, cut them in half, cut out the core, and scoop out the soft pulp.

TO SERVE

Slice wedges and serve with whipped cream to which you've added a splash of cognac and a dollop of sour cream, and a small scoop of pumpkin or persimmon sorbet or cinnamon ice cream.

TO MAKE PUMPKIN PURÉE

Preheat oven to 375°.

Slice wedges from a fresh pumpkin, preferably a sugar pie or other small version, and remove the seeds. Place the wedges on a piece of aluminum foil on a cookie sheet, add a tablespoon of butter, and seal the foil into a packet. Place the cookie sheet in the oven until the pumpkin flesh yields to the pressure of your finger. Remove from the oven and let things cool enough to handle them. Remove the skin from the pumpkin and purée the pulp in a food processor or blender. Any extra can be used for pies, sorbet or ice cream, or saved for another pudding.

BUTTERNUT SQUASH RAVIOLI with BLACK WALNUT BROWN-BUTTER SAUCE

Makes 30 ravioli

Ravioli filling ingredients

2-pound butternut squash, halved lengthwise and seeded

1 tablespoon unsalted butter

1 medium onion, chopped (about 1½ cups)

1 garlic clove, minced

5 sage leaves, finely chopped (or substitute 1½ teaspoons ground sage)

1½ teaspoons fresh thyme leaves, finely chopped (or substitute ½ teaspoon dried thyme)

½ teaspoon salt and a few grinds of black pepper

3 ounces aged goat cheese, crumbled (or substitute ricotta)

Additional ingredients

60 wonton wrappers, or gyoza or potsticker wrappers

1 stick (½ cup) unsalted butter

⅓ cup black walnuts (or English walnuts or hazelnuts), toasted lightly and chopped coarsely

TO PREPARE THE FILLING

Preheat oven to 425° and lightly grease a baking sheet.

Cut the squash in half and place it on the baking sheet, cut side down. Roast for 30 minutes, or until the flesh is very tender when you poke it with a fork. Let it cool a few minutes so you don't hurt your hands, and then scoop out the insides and throw away the skin. Place the squash in a mixing bowl and mash it with a fork.

Melt butter in a small skillet over medium heat and cook the onion, garlic, sage and thyme, stirring occasionally, for 5 minutes until the onion is golden and soft. Add salt and pepper.

Add the onion mixture to the squash along with the goat cheese and mix together with a spoon.

TO PREPARE THE RAVIOLI

Put 3 wonton wrappers on a work surface, lightly dusted with flour. Place a tablespoon of the squash filling in the center of each wrapper, and then lightly brush the perimeter with water and press a second wrapper on top, pushing out any air bubbles and sealing the edges. If you have a round ravioli cutter, you can trim the edges of the dough, but it's not necessary. Place the ravioli on a towel to dry a bit while you continue making the remaining ravioli.

In a skillet, melt the butter over medium heat and add the black walnuts. Cook until the butter begins to brown, about 3 minutes, and immediately remove the pan from the heat. Add salt and pepper and keep the black walnut butter warm and covered.

Ravioli *(continued)*

In a large pot, add 1 teaspoon of salt to 4 quarts of water and bring to a boil. Cook 10 ravioli at a time in gently boiling water for 5 minutes, or until they rise to the surface and are tender. Carefully remove cooked ravioli with a slotted spoon and place them on a plate with a small amount of the hot cooking water to keep them warm until the rest are finished.

Lift them with a slotted spoon and serve 5 to a plate, topped with the brown-butter sauce.

Wine suggestions
Riesling; Viognier

Stuffed pattypan squash

Pattypan squash are beautiful and tender when small, but seedy and fibrous when allowed to grow large. Occasionally when one gets away from us in the garden we've been known to hollow it out and use it as a vase filled with sunflowers. Then it's beautiful again.

Makes 6

6 small (2–3-inch) pattypan squash
2 tablespoons butter
¼ cup onion, minced
1 clove garlic, minced
3 ounces cream cheese
½ teaspoon salt
¼ teaspoon Tabasco sauce

Preheat oven to 350°.

Slice the squash in half through the equator. Melt the butter in a small skillet. Add the squash halves, cut-side down, and brown them slightly for 4–5 minutes. Remove the squash to a baking sheet.

Add the onion and garlic to the butter in the skillet and sauté until the garlic is lightly browned and the onion is translucent. Mix them into the cream cheese along with the salt and Tabasco sauce.

Divide the cream cheese mixture among the squashes, placing a spoonful on the bottom half. Put the top half on the cheese and wrap the stuffed squash individually in tin foil.

Bake at 350° for 20 minutes until the squash softens and yields to pressure.

GOUGÈRE – CHEESE PUFFS

Gougères are a fixture at wine tastings in Burgundy. They're best eaten right out of the oven, but can be frozen and reheated. Traditionally they're made with some sort of Swiss cheese – Emmentaler or Gruyère – and the aroma when they're baking is a taste treat all by itself. Try them with La Reve sparkling wine from Domaine Carneros, Terraces Cabernet Sauvignon, or Faila Pinot Noir.

Makes 50 puffs

1½ cups water

½ cup sweet butter, sliced into pieces

½ teaspoon salt

1½ cups flour

6 eggs

½ pound Swiss cheese of some sort or Manchego from Spain, shredded

Preheat oven to 325°.

Butter and flour 2 baking sheets or use a Silpat sheet.

Put water, butter and salt into a saucepan and bring to a boil. Once the butter melts, take the pan off the heat and add the flour all at once. Beat with a wooden spoon until thoroughly mixed.

Put the pan back on the stove over low heat (I use a screen or diffuser) and keep beating until the dough is smooth and forms a ball (about a minute).

Remove from the heat again and beat in the eggs one at a time until they lose their shine and you get a dough that's soft but will hold its shape. Stir in the shredded cheese.

Use a small ice cream scoop to put 1-inch balls on the baking sheets, an inch or two apart.

Bake for 5 minutes at 325° and then increase the heat to 375° and bake until golden and crisp – 30 to 40 minutes.

Moroccan Excursion

A little morocco-chocco

Everything begins with tea

Chocolate mint tea

Watermelon and feta salad

Tajine of kefta and eggs

With tajine, you get couscous

Chocolate-filled gazelle horns

Tajine of eggs baked with summer vegetables

Fruity couscous

everything begins with tea

CHOCOLATE MINT TEA

A basic ingredient of Moroccan hospitality, mint tea is served before a meal, during and after, while you're thinking of purchasing a rug, consummating the purchase of an antique, when welcomed into someone's home…No important – or trivial – social or business occasion is complete without sweet mint tea. It is generally poured from a great height into glasses. In Timbuktu, they serve tea three times from the pot. It becomes progressively stronger: the second cup is considered the best, and the third can remove the enamel from your teeth.

We grow chocolate mint in the garden. It smells like those little after-dinner mints that come wrapped in green foil. Plants are available at any garden center with a decent selection of herbs. Once planted, like most mints, it will grow forever, or until you put a stake through its heart, so put it in the garden in a location where you don't mind if it takes over the neighborhood. It also grows well in a pot.

Makes 1 teapot

1 bunch fresh chocolate mint – approximately 1 cup of leaves

1 teaspoon dried mint tea (loose tea, not from a teabag)

Sugar to taste

Place the fresh mint in the bottom of the teapot and crush the leaves with a thick dowel or wooden spoon. (If you were making a mint julep, this would be called muddling.) Add the dried mint tea and then fill the pot with boiling water. Let it steep for 5 minutes before serving.

"Researchers have discovered that chocolate produces some of the same reactions in the brain as marijuana. The researchers also discovered other similarities between the two, but can't remember what they are."
Matt Lauer, NBC's Today Show

WATERMELON and FETA SALAD

A wake-up call to your tastebuds: sweet, sour, spicy, cool, crunchy, salty – this salad has it all.

3 cups watermelon, cut into 1-inch cubes

1 large shallot, finely chopped

Juice from 1 lime

2 cups crumbled feta cheese (½ pound)

¼ teaspoon (approximate) cayenne pepper

½ teaspoon powdered chocolate

½ teaspoon salt

Place the watermelon chunks in a beautiful bowl. Lightly toss the shallot, lime juice and feta together and then toss them with the watermelon. Sprinkle the cayenne, chocolate and salt over the top and toss lightly. Cover the bowl with a plate or plastic wrap and chill it for at least half an hour or up to 2 or 3 hours before serving.

Hint: To get the most juice out of a lime, first microwave it on high for 10 seconds.

TAJINE of KEFTA and EGGS

From the first bite of this dish I knew I had to bring it back to our guests, so we embarked on the Great Kefta Quest, traveling across Morocco in search of the tastiest version. Familiar with all aspects of Moroccan culture, our gentle guide, Chaal Houssein, introduced us to chefs and spice markets from Marrakech to Fez, and invited us to his home where his wife and mother prepared a show-stopping lunch to illustrate techniques and flavors. Most chefs were happy to share information about method and equipment, but very secretive about their spice mixtures, called *ras-al-hanout*. For me, experimenting to develop the right combination is part of the joy of reliving the sensory memories of travel – the unique flavors, scents and textures. Here's my not-so-secret translation.

Serves 8

Kefta ingredients

1½ pounds ground lamb or beef or combination of both
2 tablespoons canola or olive oil
1 large yellow onion, finely chopped
2 cloves of garlic, minced
1 bunch of parsley, discard stems and mince leaves
1 bunch of cilantro including stems, minced
¼ cup of fresh mint leaves, minced

1 teaspoon freshly ground cumin
2 teaspoons paprika
½ teaspoon cayenne
1 teaspoon cinnamon
½ teaspoon powdered ginger
1 teaspoon salt

Wine suggestions
Syrah; Sangiovese

TO MAKE THE KEFTA

Special equipment: A tajine, or substitute a 10–12-inch round baking dish with a cover.

Mince the meat, oil, onion, garlic and fresh herbs twice through a meat grinder, or pulse in a food processor. Knead in the spices and leave the mixture to stand for at least an hour to allow the flavors to marry.

Make into small meatballs, about the diameter of a quarter, by rolling a pinch of meat around in your palms. You can do this as the sauce is cooking.

TO MAKE THE SAUCE

In a tajine or baking dish over medium heat, melt the butter and add all of the sauce ingredients. Bring to a boil, then turn down the heat and simmer the sauce for 5–10 minutes until it has thickened slightly. If you drag a wooden spoon across the bottom of the pan through the sauce, you'll notice the oil will separate from the tomato liquid. At this point, add the meatballs and cook, uncovered, over gentle heat for an additional 10 minutes, turning the meatballs now and then to coat them with the sauce.

TO FINISH

Once the meatballs are cooked through, crack and drop the eggs into the sauce between the meatballs. Cover the tajine and continue to cook over medium heat until the egg whites are opaque and the yolks soft, which will only take 5–6 minutes. Sprinkle a little finely chopped parsley over the top.

Hint: Peeling and seeding tomatoes the easy way – *cut the tomato in half from the top stem end to the bottom. Scoop out the seeds with your finger without being too fussy. This is a rustic dish and a few seeds won't hurt. Place a cheese grater with medium-sized holes in a bowl. Cup the tomato in your hand with the skin-side against your palm. Run the cut side of the tomato back and forth against the grater. You'll wind up with a bowl full of crushed tomato and an empty skin in your hand.*

Sauce ingredients

2 tablespoons butter

2 pounds fresh tomatoes, peeled, seeded and diced (see *Hint*)

1 sweet red pepper

1 jalapeño pepper

1 tablespoon paprika

½ teaspoon ground cumin

½ teaspoon cinnamon

½ teaspoon salt

¼ cup water

Ingredients to finish

8 large eggs

2 tablespoons finely chopped fresh parsley

Alternative spices

Ras-al-hanout is a spice mixture that vaguely translates 'as head of the house.' Each Moroccan restaurant or cook will create a unique mixture of up to 20 spices. Available at ethnic shops or from Whole Spice (see *Resources*), *ras-al-hanout* can be substituted for the spices in this recipe, and will add an additional depth of flavor. Omit the paprika, cumin, ginger and cinnamon and use 1 tablespoon of *ras-al-hanout* in the meatballs and 2 teaspoons in the sauce.

Night owl instructions

Prepare the kefta mixture and the sauce the night before and refrigerate them separately. In the morning, reheat the sauce, roll the meatballs and add them to the sauce, followed by the eggs.

CHOCOLATE-FILLED GAZELLE HORNS

These crescent-shaped treats are a popular tradition in Morocco and Tunisia, and we tasted similar cookies in Senegal. Although generally made with almonds, occasionally pine nuts are substituted. Chocolate nibs, with their nut-like character, seemed a natural evolution.

Makes 18 cookies

Filling ingredients

1½ cups chocolate nibs

½ cup sugar

1 teaspoon cinnamon

2 tablespoons orange flower water, or substitute water flavored with ⅛ teaspoon vanilla

Dough ingredients

1⅓ cups flour

2 tablespoons vegetable oil

¼ cup orange flower water mixed with ½ cup water

Confectioner's sugar for dusting

Preheat oven to 350°.

Grind the chocolate nibs in a spice grinder, blender or mortar and pestle. Add the sugar and cinnamon and orange flower water. Mix the dough with your hands; their warmth will help the filling come together. Divide the filling into 18 pieces and roll each into a 3-inch long lozenge-shape with tapered ends.

Mix the dough ingredients in a bowl and then knead until the dough becomes smooth and pliable. Roll out the dough so that it's quite thin, about ⅛ inch. Cut it into 3-inch-wide strips.

Place the filling lozenges along the edge of the dough and brush water around the filling. Fold the dough over the filling, pressing down to seal the edges. You'll now have lumpy strips 1½-inches wide. Starting at the folded edge, cut a semicircle around the lumps of filling with a pastry cutter or a knife. Place the cookies on a greased or Silpat-covered cookie sheet, curving the ends into a crescent shape. Bake for 20–22 minutes until barely browned in a 350° oven. Dust with confectioner's sugar.

Note: *Orange flower water is available in gourmet shops, through spice vendors and in the grocery aisle in shops that cater to Moroccan, Turkish and Middle Eastern clientele. See Resources.*

TAJINE of EGGS BAKED with SUMMER VEGETABLES

Before visiting Morocco, I'd always thought of it as African and exotic. After visiting, we decided it was very Mediterranean – and still quite exotic. As a southern coastal country on the Mediterranean Sea, it shares a similar climate to Spain, Portugal, Italy and the south of France. Eggplant, zucchini, tomatoes, many varieties of peppers and olive oil all play a part in the cuisine of each country. The significant difference in flavor is from the spices. Moroccans were major players in the spice route and took their pick from all parts of the world.

This dish is a Moroccan version of ratatouille, with eggs added when the vegetables are tender and moist. The eggs absorb all of those wonderful flavors as they cook and thicken the juices from the vegetables.

Special equipment: Traditionally this dish would be cooked in a tajine over a canoon (see *Moroccan Cooking Implements* below). If you don't have either, use a large skillet, brazier or heat-proof casserole dish and cook on your stove-top, or on a charcoal grill with a slow fire. If using a ceramic tajine, place a heat diffuser under it when cooking on a stove-top.

Place the olive oil in the bottom of the tajine over medium heat.

Add the sliced onions and cook until soft and golden. Stir in the garlic, peppers and zucchini.

Holding the skin side of a tomato-half in your palm, scrape the open side against the large holes of a grater. This will release all of the pulp and juices and leave the skin in your hand. Throw the skin away. Continue with the rest of the tomatoes and add the crushed tomatoes to the vegetables in the tajine. Place the top on the tajine and cook for 15–20 minutes until the vegetables are soft and tender.

Stir in the herbs and spices, salt and pepper and cook for an additional 5 minutes.

Pour the beaten eggs over the vegetable mixture and stir. Replace the tajine lid and cook for another 10–12 minutes, until the eggs reach the consistency of soft-scrambled eggs. Sprinkle a little fresh parsley over the top and serve with couscous.

MOROCCAN COOKING IMPLEMENTS

Chaal, our wonder-guide in Morocco (see *Resources*) sent me the traditional tajine and canoon that can be found in every home and market. Together they create a portable kitchen. The tajine is the cooking pot and the canoon is essentially a Moroccan hibachi.

A glazed earthenware deep dish with a conical top, the tajine acts as a baking dish and casserole. The top allows moisture to collect and then rain down on the simmering food, keeping it moist and basted. The canoon is made of unglazed earthenware and has a raised bowl-like base where a charcoal fire is created. When the flames have subsided and the coals are perfect and gray, the tajine is placed on supports surrounding the fire, and cooking commences.

Tajines in different sizes and styles are readily available in cooking supply shops like Williams-Sonoma or Sur la Table. For the traditional version and a canoon, search out a Moroccan or Tunisian shop or contact Chaal, the next best thing to visiting Morocco.

Serves 8

⅓ cup olive oil
1 large yellow onion, sliced
6 crushed garlic cloves
4 red bell peppers, seeded and diced into ½-inch pieces
4 red jalapeños (or substitute green) seeded, membranes removed, and minced
2 serrano chiles, seeded and minced
2 yellow zucchini, sliced into ½-inch-thick rounds
8 ripe tomatoes, halved from stem end to bottom
1 tablespoon harissa, optional, but oh so good (see *Pantry,* page 270)

2 tablespoons cilantro, chopped
2 tablespoons parsley, chopped and a little extra for garnish
1 teaspoon paprika
1 teaspoon freshly ground cumin
1 teaspoon salt
freshly ground pepper to taste

8 eggs, beaten

Night owl instructions and camping-out Moroccan style

Traditionally cooked in a tajine over a charcoal fire, this is a great dish to prepare on a camping trip. All of the slicing and dicing can be done the night before and then assembled and cooked in the morning, or when you reach your campsite.

Wine suggestions
Rosé; Pinot Noir

FRUITY COUSCOUS

Ground cherries are small fruit about half the size of a cherry but unrelated. They're covered with a papery husk, much like a tomatillo, but with a sweeter tangier taste, and grow in South America, Africa and all over the U.S., including our garden in Napa. Our friend Siga mentioned that he grew up with them in Fiji. Always on the lookout for an exotic recipe, I asked what Fijians did with them. He very carefully peeled one, placed it in the center of his palm, and then smacked himself in the forehead with it. Personally, I prefer it in couscous. If you don't have access to them, they can be omitted from this recipe, and you could always smack yourself in the forehead with a grape instead.

Serves 6

5 tablespoons olive oil

1½ teaspoons ground cinnamon

1½ teaspoons ground coriander

½ teaspoon ground cloves

1½ teaspoons ground cumin

2 tablespoons brown sugar

¼ cup pine nuts

2 tablespoons lemon juice

¼ cup chopped cilantro leaves

½ cup dried cranberries

½ cup raisins

½ cup halved ground cherries (also called Cape gooseberries or physallis), optional

3 cups chicken stock

2 cups couscous

1 teaspoon salt

A few grindings of fresh black pepper

Heat the olive oil in a saucepan over medium heat. Add the spices, sugar and pine nuts and stir for a minute or two. Add the lemon juice, cilantro, fruit and stock. Bring to a boil. Stir in the couscous and salt and pepper, cover the pan and remove it from the heat. Stir occasionally with a fork. It will stay warm for half an hour.

When ready to serve, mound in a bowl and decorate with stripes of cinnamon.

All-American

As American as chocolate pie

A little sandwich to take the edge off
Chocolate sandwich
Herbed scrambled eggs over roasted portabello mushroom

———

General Custard meets his match
Banana ice cream sandwiches with coffee caramelized bananas
Corn custard and tomato fritters

———

New malt shop favorites
Marc's marvelous chocolate milkshake
Papaya mousse parfait
Chocolate brownie macadamia nut waffle with Bellini peaches

———

Reverse breakfast
Mini toast, hash browns and sunny side-up quail eggs
Chocolate omelet with blueberries in a Pinot Noir sauce

———

Not your average diner menu
Baby banana split
Red, white and blue pancakes

———

When extravangence is the object
Chocolate truffle fritters with cherry sauce
Scrambled eggs with lobster, mascarpone, caviar and scallops

———

Autumn approaches, can winter be far behind?
Poached apples in chocolate gingerbread cookie cups
Rolled ricotta omelet with cheesy potato cakes

———

Starting the year properly
Raspberry soufflé
Poppers for two
Cheddar cheese surprise muffins

CHOCOLATE SANDWICH

A thick slice of this chocolate bread can stand on its own as a first course served with fresh fruit and a scoop of sorbet. Or make the sandwiches and serve them with the blood orange soup on page 222 for a soup and a sandwich menu.

Makes 4 small loaf pans

Ingredients for chocolate bread

2 cups flour
1 cup cocoa
1 teaspoon baking powder
½ teaspoon baking soda
1 teaspoon salt
1½ cups softened butter
2 ¾ cups sugar
2 teaspoons vanilla
2 teaspoons espresso or strong coffee
5 eggs
1¼ cups buttermilk

Chocolate sandwich fillings

Cream cheese
Peanut butter
Fruit jam or jelly
Hot pepper jelly
Cabernet Sauvignon jelly

TO MAKE THE BREAD

Preheat oven to 325°. Sift the flour, cocoa, baking powder, baking soda and salt together. Put the butter in a mixing bowl and beat it until it's creamy. Add the sugar and beat again until it's fluffy. Add the vanilla, espresso and the eggs, one by one, beating just until they're incorporated.

Add ⅓ of the flour mixture and ½ cup of the buttermilk and beat them into the batter. Repeat until all of the flour and the last ¼ cup of buttermilk are blended into a smooth mixture.

Brush 4 small loaf pans (6 x 3½ x 2½ inches deep) with butter. Pour sugar into the pans and swirl them around so that the sugar coats the surface. Turn the pans upside-down so any extra sugar falls out.

Ladle the batter into the loaf pans and bake for 45–50 minutes until the top springs back when you tap it.

Cool the loaves for half an hour in the pan on a wire rack. Then tip them out of the pan and cool the rest of the way on the rack. To make slicing easier, wrap in aluminum foil and freeze briefly before making the sandwiches.

TO MAKE THE CHOCOLATE SANDWICHES

Slice the chocolate bread ¼-inch thick, using a serrated knife.

Spread cream cheese or peanut butter on a slice of the chocolate bread and top with jam or jelly and another piece of bread. Slice the sandwich in half and secure it with a decorative pick.

Buttermilk substitute

If you don't have any buttermilk, you can substitute plain yogurt or sour cream (not the fat-free stuff). Or, to make pretend buttermilk, add 1¾ tablespoons of cream of tartar to a cup of milk, or add a tablespoon of lemon juice or white vinegar to a cup of milk and let it stand for 5–10 minutes.

HERBED SCRAMBLED EGGS over ROASTED PORTABELLO MUSHROOM

Serves 8

8 medium portabello mushrooms

2 large garlic cloves

½ cup extra virgin olive oil

16 large eggs

3 tablespoons half-and-half

3 tablespoons butter

⅔ cup ricotta cheese

¼ cup chopped basil

3 tablespoons aged balsamic vinegar (if you can't find aged, reduce a young balsamic by half to intensify the flavor)

1 large ripe tomato, or 3 plum tomatoes, seeded and diced (½-inch)

Polenta cakes, recipe follows (should be made the day before)

Preheat oven to 375°.

Choose firm, blemish-free portabellos without black gills on the underside. Remove the stems from the mushrooms. Chop the garlic and mix it with the olive oil and let it sit for a few minutes to infuse the oil a bit. Brush both sides of each mushroom with the oil and place them on a cookie sheet in the preheated oven for 15 minutes until just cooked. They'll soften and begin to exude some liquid.

Whisk the eggs and half-and-half together. Melt the butter in a large skillet over medium heat. When the butter sizzles, add the eggs and stir until they are soft and glossy. Stir in the ricotta cheese and continue cooking for 2 more minutes. Remove the eggs from the heat and stir in the basil.

Place mushrooms, undersides up, on each plate. Sprinkle with the balsamic vinegar and spoon the egg mixture into the mushrooms, trailing some of it over one side. Garnish with chopped tomatoes and serve with 2 or 3 pieces of grilled polenta.

1½ cups polenta (not instant polenta and definitely not cornmeal)

1 cup fontina cheese

6 cups water

1 tablespoon salt

2 tablespoons butter

½ to 1 cup grated Parmesan, to taste

Wine suggestions
Pinot Noir; Cabernet Franc

POLENTA CAKES

The polenta should be made the day before. If preparing the polenta beforehand doesn't fit your schedule, substitute a couple of slices of toasted baguette brushed with melted butter, sprinkled with Parmesan and lightly warmed in the oven at the same time you're cooking the portabellos.

Bring water and salt to a boil. Gradually pour in the polenta, stirring continuously until thickened. Cook over a low heat for about 20 minutes (if you have a heat diffuser this would be a good time to use it). Stir occasionally to prevent sticking. If it starts to look dry, just add a bit more water. When finished, add the fontina and Parmesan to taste, then pour the polenta into two 8 x 5-inch oiled loaf pans. Set aside until cool, then cover with plastic wrap and place in the refrigerator.

Before starting your eggs, remove the polenta from the refrigerator and remove it from the pan. Heat a grill pan or preheat the broiler. Slice the polenta ½-inch thick, brush with olive oil and grill over medium-high heat until well marked and warmed through. If broiling, you just want the polenta to brown around the edges.

BANANA ICE CREAM SANDWICHES with COFFEE CARAMELIZED BANANAS

"Locavore," the new ugly term for a good idea, conjures up images of pigs snuffling along the ground looking for edibles. Unhappily, the word is used to describe those of us who eat and serve food that's local and in season. That makes for great food and responsible use of resources, but most of us don't live in the tropics and, sometimes, you just need a banana. Particularly in the winter, when local fruit is scarce, we yearn for that comforting soft sweetness. Combined with chocolate and warm coffee, these banana sandwiches will brighten any winter morning.

Serves 6

Cookie ingredients
½ cup butter, softened
⅔ cup sugar
1 egg
1 teaspoon vanilla
1½ cups flour
6 tablespoons cocoa
½ teaspoon baking soda
¼ teaspoon salt

CHOCOLATE COOKIES

Special equipment: A 1¾-inch round cookie cutter.

Thoroughly blend the butter and sugar in a mixing bowl, and then add the egg and vanilla. Beat until combined. Sift the dry ingredients together and then add them to the batter. Stir until the batter is completely incorporated.

Place the resulting dough onto a large piece of plastic wrap and roll it into a cylinder about 2 inches in diameter. Place it in the refrigerator until it gets firm – half an hour or more.

When the dough is solid, preheat the oven to 350°.

Cut the cookie dough into 26 ³⁄₁₆-inch slices (you'll need to nosh on one warm cookie and may need the other as a back-up). Place them on a greased cookie sheet or Silpat sheet. Bake for 8–10 minutes. Remove the cookies from the oven. They will be slightly irregular, so trim them into perfect circles with a 1¾-inch round cookie cutter. Set aside.

4 tablespoons butter

**2 vanilla beans, split (or substitute
    2 teaspoons of pure vanilla extract)**

1½ cups brown sugar

1½ cups strong coffee

6 ripe but firm bananas

**Banana sorbet (see *Frozen Delights*,
    page 261)**

COFFEE CARAMELIZED BANANAS

Melt the butter, brown sugar and vanilla beans together until well-combined. Add the coffee and lightly boil the mixture until it has reduced and is a bit syrupy. Set aside.

When you're ready to serve, slice the bananas into the warm sauce and then immediately spoon over the sandwiches.

TO ASSEMBLE

Remove the banana sorbet from the freezer and let it sit for 20 minutes or so to soften. Using a small ice cream scoop, place a tablespoon of sorbet on the flat side of a cookie. Top with another cookie, placing the flat side against the sorbet, and press the sandwich together, smoothing the sorbet on the sides. Repeat with the remaining cookies to make 12 sandwiches.

Put the sandwiches back in the freezer while you re-warm the coffee syrup. Turn off the heat and add the bananas (don't cook them). Retrieve your sandwiches from the freezer and place two on each plate, putting one on its side and the other one flat, then spoon the bananas and sauce over and around the sandwiches. A scoop of orange sorbet as garnish will add a bit of acidity as contrast.

*"Chocolate is nature's way of
making up for Mondays."*

CORN CUSTARD and TOMATO FRITTERS

If my kitchen compatriot, Shirlee, were to write a breakfast cookbook, it would probably be titled Corn for Breakfast – and Lunch and Dinner. It's her Nebraska upbringing, no doubt, surrounded by all of those cornfields. When sweet corn is in season and the tomatoes are ripe she's a happy gal – and so are we when she makes this silky sensuous custard, paired with crispy tomato fritters. And if you like corn as much as she does, try the corn fritters for a crispy-silky corn contrast.

Serves 6

Custard ingredients

2 tablespoons butter
2 or 3 ears fresh sweet corn kernels, cut off the cob
1 medium red bell pepper, diced
6 scallions, chopped
½ teaspoon salt
Freshly ground pepper to taste
4 tablespoons fresh basil, chopped or 2 tablespoons dried basil

4 ounces creamy goat cheese
6 eggs
1½ cups cream (you can substitute half-and-half, milk or some combination thereof, but then add another egg)
Salt and pepper to taste

2 ounces grated Parmesan

Alternative: Sauté wild mushrooms, especially chanterelles, with the vegetable mixture.

GOAT CHEESE AND CORN CUSTARD

Corn mixture: Melt the butter in a skillet over medium heat and sauté the corn and peppers just until the peppers are slightly softened, 5–7 minutes. Toss in the scallions and season with salt, pepper and basil. Set aside.

Custard: Blend goat cheese, eggs and cream in a food processor until thoroughly mixed. Season with salt and pepper and set aside.

TO BAKE

Preheat oven to 375°. Butter or spray six 8-ounce ramekins with oil and place them in a baking pan.

Divide the corn mixture evenly into the dishes. Sprinkle the Parmesan cheese on top and then ladle the custard mixture over that. Fill the baking pan with enough boiling water to come halfway up the sides of the ramekins, creating a water bath, also called a bain marie. This helps to cook the custard evenly and keep it creamy.

Place the pan in the center of the preheated oven and bake for 35–45 minutes or until the custard is set and no longer liquid. It will be lightly browned.

Remove the ramekins from the water bath and cool for a few minutes. The custard can be served in the ramekins or can be turned out onto a serving plate and served with the corn on top by holding a plate firmly over the ramekin and turning it upside down.

Fresh tomato fritter ingredients (makes 24)

5 large fresh tomatoes from the garden or farmers' market, halved, or substitute 24 ounces canned tomatoes, drained and roughly chopped (use Mexican-style tomatoes if they're available)

¼ cup fresh chopped basil (omit if using canned and flavored tomatoes)

1 cup flour

1 teaspoon baking powder

1 teaspoon sugar

¾ teaspoon salt

1 tablespoon grated yellow onion

1 egg

Oil for frying

Corn fritter ingredients (makes 24)

3 or 4 ears fresh corn

1 cup milk

1½ cups flour

1 tablespoon baking powder

¾ teaspoon salt

1 beaten egg

¾ teaspoon oregano (optional)

Oil for frying

Wine suggestions
Chardonnay; rich Sauvignon Blanc; Albariño

FRESH TOMATO FRITTERS

Equipment: A deep skillet with 2 inches of vegetable or peanut oil or a deep-fryer.

Squeeze a tomato-half slightly to remove some of the liquid and seeds. Place the skin of the tomato-half in your hand and grate it through the large holes on a box grater. Discard the skin.

Blend the tomatoes with the rest of the ingredients to create a batter. Mix just until the flour is incorporated.

Heat oil to 350°. Drop teaspoons of batter into the oil and cook for approximately 4 minutes, turning once during cooking. Drain on paper and serve.

CORN FRITTERS

Heat 2–3 inches of oil in a large pan to 350° while you're mixing the batter.

Remove kernels from the cobs and mix them with the liquid ingredients. Then add to the dry ingredients. Stir just until the flour is moistened.

Drop the batter by teaspoons into the hot oil. Cook for 2–3 minutes on each side or until golden. Drain on paper towels. Serve with fresh tomato salsa, 5-chile ketchup (see *Pantry*, page 274), or an avocado or tomatillo salsa.

MARC'S MARVELOUS CHOCOLATE MILKSHAKE

It must be told. Marc Hoberman has a serious chocolate milkshake addiction. Incurable, in fact, and it mirrors his disdain for Champagne and wine. To avoid embarrassment (ours, not his), as we left for the world-renowned *French Laundry* restaurant, we called ahead to alert them to his affliction. When John and I were served a glass of bubbly, a perfect chocolate shake was delivered with great ceremony to Marc. The courageous waiter walked past two young boys at the next table, and despite their stares, Marc consumed his treat in the most leisurely manner over the course of a 4-hour meal. Reportedly it was the first time such a concoction has graced the Robot Coupe food processor in the restaurant's kitchen.

Determined to create the perfect shake, the next day we scoured the market for all manner of ice cream, chocolate syrup, candies, cookies and anything else that Marc placed on the conveyor belt before I slapped his hand. Back at the Inn, we loaded the Robot Coupe, whirred and tasted, never quite getting it right – until I reached into the cooled pot of chocolate fondue we'd just photographed, put a huge dollop into vanilla ice cream, and that was it! The finishing touch, for a tiny French nod, is a sprinkling of Le Petit Écolier cookie crumbs on top.

¼ cup cream

4 ounces bittersweet chocolate, chopped into small pieces

1 tablespoon cognac or brandy

1 pint best quality vanilla ice cream

1 Le Petit Écolier cookie crumbled

Bring the cream to a boil in a small saucepan. Pour it in a bowl over the chopped chocolate. Whisk until velvety smooth. Add the cognac and let the mixture cool slightly. The good news is that there will be extra because it's difficult to boil a smaller amount of cream without burning it. Keep the remainder in the refrigerator (if you can).

Take 2 heaped tablespoons of the chocolate mixture and add it to the ice cream in a food processor. Blend. Taste to determine if more chocolate is needed. Spoon the shake into a beautiful Champagne glass. Top with cookie crumbs and serve with a wide straw.

PAPAYA MOUSSE PARFAIT

This could also be called the whatever's-in-the-market parfait. Replace the papaya with mangoes or bananas, if those are readily available, or peaches and nectarines in the summer. Use whatever berries are grown in your area. A kiwi adds a sweet-tart note and its black-seeded green beauty.

Serves 8

¼ cup orange juice

splash of cognac

2 cups of berries – strawberries, raspberries, boysenberries… whatever is in season

1 medium-sized papaya

¼ cup fresh lemon juice

Pinch salt

¼ cup sugar

2 cups strained non-fat yogurt

½ cup whipped cream (optional)

1 kiwi, peeled and sliced

Hint: *Place the yogurt in a strainer lined with cheese cloth and let it drain overnight in the refrigerator until it reaches a thick cheese-like consistency.*

Mix orange juice and cognac in a bowl big enough to hold the berries. Marinate the berries for a ½ hour in the orange juice-cognac mixture.

Peel the papaya. Scoop out and discard the seeds. Purée the papaya in a food processor or blender with the lemon juice, salt and sugar. Add the yogurt and blend until smooth. Taste and add more sugar if necessary. Fold in the whipped cream if you're using it.

Spoon the papaya mousse into dessert or parfait glasses, alternating mousse with the marinated berries. Garnish with a scoop of fruit sorbet, a mint sprig and your favorite chocolate cookie.

CHOCOLATE BROWNIE MACADAMIA NUT WAFFLE with BELLINI PEACHES

I'm not a big fan of waffles. They're often bland, mushy and only a slightly better vehicle for eating maple syrup and butter than a piece of corrugated cardboard. But it seemed as though a chocolate breakfast cookbook should have a waffle recipe, so we experimented (and experimented and experimented – and I apologize to everyone for how grumpy it made me) and finally came up with two that meet the test of good flavor when eaten plain. Of course, they're even better when paired with fruit and the occasional scoop of ice cream or sorbet. Or served with crème anglaise. Or chocolate syrup. Or cognac-laced melted butter. So OK, maybe waffles aren't that bad.

The chocolate banana version is in the Valentine's section, page 210. Those waffles are thin and slightly crispy and best made as soon as the batter is prepared. These brownie macadamia waffles are more forgiving, so are the ones to make with unruly guests who appear at the breakfast table at uneven intervals.

Waffle ingredients

4 ounces bittersweet chocolate
½ cup (1 stick) of butter, melted
3 eggs
½ cup sugar
1 teaspoon vanilla
½ teaspoon salt
1½ cups flour
¾ cup chopped macadamia nuts
½ to ¾ cup milk

Bellini peach ingredients

4 perfect white peaches
1 glass Champagne (6 ounces or so)
2 tablespoons butter
1 tablespoon brown sugar

TO MAKE THE WAFFLES

Preheat the waffle-maker.

Place the chocolate and butter in the top pan of a double boiler over boiling water. Once the chocolate starts melting, stir until you have a smooth mixture. Remove from the heat.

In a mixing bowl, beat the eggs with the sugar until pale and fluffy. Mix in the vanilla and salt. Add the chocolate mixture and combine well. Stir in the flour, nuts and half of the milk. Continue adding just enough milk to make a thick batter. Spoon (it will be too thick to pour) ⅓ cup of batter onto the hot waffle-maker. Close the lid and cook until done.

TO MAKE THE BELLINI PEACHES

Harry's Bar in Venice is famous for its Bellinis, a sparkling drink made with Prosecco and white peach juice. When white peaches are in season, we serve them every way we can.

Peel and slice the peaches into a bowl and top with a glass of Champagne. Melt the butter in a skillet over medium-high heat. Lift the peaches from the bowl with a slotted spoon and sauté them quickly in the butter. Remove to another bowl. Pour the Champagne and any accumulated peach juice into the skillet and add the brown sugar. Stir until the sugar melts and the mixture bubbles and turns a lovely caramel color. Pour the caramel over the peaches, stir gently and serve over the waffles. Add a dollop of whipped cream and a few raspberries.

Night owl instructions

The batter can be made the night before and kept in the refrigerator. Add a splash of milk if it needs to be thinned out a little in the morning.

MINI TOAST, HASH BROWNS and SUNNY SIDE-UP QUAIL EGGS

When a fruit dish is substantial enough to deserve main course treatment, we reverse the normal sequence and start with a savory dish. The first course is a miniature version of a diner breakfast of sunny side-up eggs, hash browned potatoes and toast. To keep all of the ingredients in proportion, mince the onions finely and cut the potatoes into small dice. If quail eggs are not available, scramble some chicken eggs or make a miniature cheese omelet to add to the dish. As a lifelong stalker of kitchen supply stores, I have a collection of small skillets which I use to serve this dish. If you're not similarly possessed and equipped, serve the breakfast on a small plate.

serves 6

Hash brown ingredients

1 tablespoon oil
1 tablespoon butter
½ onion, finely chopped
3 potatoes – Yukon gold, red bliss, Peruvian blue, or combination
¼ cup chopped sweet red pepper
1 serrano or cayenne chile, minced
½ teasoon salt, or more, to taste
Freshly ground pepper

Additional ingredients

1 tablespoon butter
18 quail eggs
12 slices of cocktail-sized bread, toasted and buttered

TO PREPARE THE HASH BROWN POTATOES

Peel the potatoes and cut into small (¼-inch) cubes.

Place the oil and melt the butter in a skillet over medium heat. Add the onion and sauté until softened but not brown. Stir in the potatoes, lower the heat and cover the pan for 10 minutes to cook the potatoes through. Add the peppers and turn the heat back up to medium to lightly brown the potatoes, stirring occasionally.

TO PREPARE THE QUAIL EGGS

Melt butter in a skillet over medium heat until hot and foamy, but not browned. Quail eggs don't crack easily as they have a strong membrane under the shell. Slice the wider end off the egg with a serrated knife. Pour the egg out of the shell into the foaming butter and fry until the white is firm and yolk still runny. Flip once over-easy if you prefer.

Serve on the hash browns with a side of toast.

CHOCOLATE OMELET with BLUEBERRIES in a PINOT NOIR SAUCE

Serves 8

Omelet batter ingredients

¾ cup flour

1 tablespoon sugar

¼ teaspoon salt

Zest of an orange, grated – just the orange skin, not the bitter white pith underneath

1 stick (½ cup) butter, melted

3 eggs, beaten slightly

½ teaspoon vanilla

1 cup milk

Optional: 2 tablespoons Cointreau, or substitute Grand Marnier or other orange liqueur

This recipe makes enough extra batter that you don't need to worry about having a couple of unsuccessful attempts before you get the technique and temperature adjusted.

TO MAKE THE OMELET BATTER

Blend flour, sugar, salt and orange zest in a mixing bowl. Add melted butter and mix. Then add eggs, then vanilla, milk and liqueur. Mix until smooth.

Heat a crêpe pan or a small (6-inch or so) frying pan over medium-high heat. When you hold your hand 2–3 inches over the pan and can feel the heat, it's ready. Pour ⅓ cup of the batter into the pan and swirl it to coat the bottom with a 5–6-inch circle. Cook until the edges get dry. Lift it with a knife and peek underneath to see if it's slightly browned. Then turn and cook the other side until it's browned, too. The result is sort of an eggy-crêpe. If you're not going to use them right away, separate with waxed paper, cover with plastic wrap and place in the refrigerator.

Chocolate filling ingredients

2 egg whites

3 egg yolks, one at a time

5 ounces of whole milk, heated

1 teaspoon vanilla

2 tablespoons butter

⅓ cup flour – sieved

¼ cup sugar

2 ounces bittersweet chocolate, melted

1 teaspoon balsamic vinegar

Grated zest of ½ orange

Blueberry sauce ingredients

3 tablespoons butter

3 tablespoons brown sugar

½ teaspoon freshly grated nutmeg

1 cup Pinot Noir (or Cabernet or Zinfandel)

1 cup fresh blueberries

TO MAKE THE CHOCOLATE FILLING

Separate the eggs and let them come to room temperature. Put 2 whites in an immaculately clean mixing bowl (saving the other white for another purpose) and put the yolks in a separate small bowl. Try to avoid breaking the yolks, but the world won't come to an end if you do.

Heat the milk to a simmer with the vanilla. (You can do this in a pyrex measuring cup in the microwave, or on top of the stove in a pan.) Set aside for a few minutes while you…

In a separate medium-sized saucepan, melt the butter. Add flour and stir vigorously with a wooden spoon. Add the warm vanilla-milk all at once and stir enthusiastically. It will be a bit lumpy and the consistency of paste. Don't lose heart, just keep stirring and the lumps will disappear.

Add one egg yolk, stirring until it's thoroughly incorporated and the mixture loses its shine. Then add the next one. And the next. Now stir in the melted chocolate, balsamic vinegar and the orange zest. Set aside while you…

Turn on the mixer to medium-high to start beating the whites. Once they begin to thicken and become opaque, add the ¼ cup sugar. Continue beating until they're fairly stiff so that when you pull the beaters out, the whites follow and make peaks. Stir about ¼ of the egg whites into the chocolate mixture. This loosens up the batter so that it will be easier to add the rest of the egg whites. Fold the whites in gently so that no white is visible. The filling is now ready and can be refrigerated if you're not going to use it right away.

TO MAKE THE BLUEBERRY SAUCE

Melt the butter in a small saucepan. Add the brown sugar and stir until it melts. Add nutmeg and wine and simmer over medium-high heat for 5–10 minutes to reduce the mixture and concentrate the flavors. Take the pan off the heat and add the blueberries. (If you're making the sauce ahead of time, don't add the berries until you reheat the sauce just before serving.)

TO ASSEMBLE

2 tablespoons butter, melted

Place 2–3 tablespoons of the chocolate mixture in the middle of each omelet. Fold in half to enclose the filling and create a half-moon-shaped omelet. Continue with the others and put them on a buttered baking sheet. Brush each omelet with the butter and place in the oven for 8 minutes at 400° until puffed.

Put a little sauce on the plate. Put the omelet on the sauce and top with some more sauce and berries. A tiny scoop of a fruit sorbet on the side makes a wonderful hot-cold contrast.

Night owl instructions

Everything except the final assemblage and baking can be done the night before. In the morning, take the omelet/crêpes, filling and sauce out of the refrigerator and let them come to room temperature. Heat the sauce, bake the omelets, add the blueberries to the sauce and serve.

BABY BANANA SPLIT

Baby bananas are actually not babies, but a full-grown separate and distinct variety. They are available at the supermarket or gourmet fruit stand. Firmer than standard bananas, they pack a lot of flavor in that small package.

Serves 4

6 baby bananas

½ cup orange juice

2 kiwi, peeled

1 tablespoon sugar

1 tablespoon lime juice (or substitute lemon juice)

⅔ cup whipped cream

¼ cup chocolate nibs

3 types of fruit sorbet

Mint sprig to garnish

Peel the bananas and cut them in half the long way. Place them in a small bowl and pour the orange juice over them. The ascorbic acid in the orange juice will keep them from turning brown.

Purée the kiwi in a food processor or blender with the sugar and lime juice.

TO ASSEMBLE

Spread ¼ of the kiwi purée on a small plate. Place 3 halves of banana on top. Dollop some whipped cream across the middle of the bananas. Besides being a necessary ingredient for a banana split, this will help keep the sorbet in place. Sprinkle the chocolate nibs over the whipped cream and bananas and top with a scoop of each of the sorbets. Garnish with a mint sprig.

RED, WHITE and BLUE PANCAKES

A staple in native southwestern cooking, blue and red cornmeal can now be purchased in most U.S. supermarkets and gourmet shops. We found out the hard way that there's something particularly appealing about blue cornmeal to kitties when our one-year-old kitten, Doctor Livingstone, landed on John's plate as he was eating breakfast one day. A red abysinnian covered with prickly pear syrup is not a pretty sight. Especially when he's running over the tablecloth and leaping off your shoulder. Be forewarned. Of course, it didn't stop John from finishing his breakfast. Not much does.

Makes 30–35 cakes

Blue cornmeal pancake ingredients

1⅓ cups blue cornmeal

2 tablespoons flour

2 tablespoons sugar

1 tablespoon baking powder

1 teaspoon salt

2 eggs, beaten

1 cup milk

¼ cup melted butter

Red cornmeal pancake ingredients

Same as above, except use red cornmeal

Piñon pancake ingredients

1½ cups shelled piñon (pine nuts)

1 cup flour

½ teaspoon salt

2 tablespoons sugar

1 cup milk

TO MAKE THE BATTER

Cornmeal pancakes: Add the dry ingredients to a mixing bowl. Mix the eggs, milk and butter together and stir into the cornmeal mixture.

Piñon pancakes: Grind the pine nuts in a blender with the flour until coarsely chopped. Don't over-blend or you'll have pine nut butter. Add the remaining ingredients and mix. Let the batter stand for an hour or so.

½ stick (4 tablespoons) melted butter for the griddle

TO PREPARE THE PANCAKES

Put a platter in a warm (250°) oven. As you cook the pancakes, place them on the platter to stay warm, with a light towel over them.

Place a griddle or large skillet over medium heat. Brush it lightly with the melted butter. Place a spoonful of the thick piñon batter onto the hot surface and press down slightly with a buttered spatula so that you create a 3-inch round, ¼ –½-inch thick cake. Repeat until you use up the batter. Do the same with the blue and red cornmeal batters, although you won't need to press them down as the batter is thinner. Butter the pan between each batch.

TO ASSEMBLE

Alternate pancakes on the plate and serve with the prickly pear syrup and mango honey. Alternatively, use maple syrup or maple butter, blueberry syrup or peach syrup.

Prickly pear syrup ingredients

12 prickly pears

¼ cup honey

1 teaspoon lime juice

PRICKLY PEAR SYRUP

Rub the outside of the prickly pears with a rough cloth to remove any remaining spines.

Cut each into quarters, leaving the skin on. Purée in a food processor or blender and press through a sieve to get rid of the skin and seeds.

Place the purée in a medium-sized saucepan over medium heat. Add the honey and juice and bring to a boil. Simmer until it thickens – 10–15 minutes. It will thicken even further as it cools.

Mango honey ingredients

1 large mango, peeled and sliced

2 tablespoons honey

1 teaspoon freshly squeezed lime juice

MANGO HONEY

Blend all ingredients in a blender or food processor.

Wine suggestions
Chardonnay; Blanc de Blanc
Sparkling Wine

CHOCOLATE TRUFFLE FRITTERS
with CHERRY SAUCE

A modern take on chocolate baked Alaska, the fritters are frozen chocolate truffles that are battered and then plunged into hot oil for the briefest moment to crisp the coating. Guests have been known to swoon.

Serves 8

Cherry sauce ingredients

1½ cups Port (we use either Jessup Cellars or Chase Family Cellars Zinfandel Port)
1 pound pitted, sweet cherries
Sugar, if needed
1–2 teaspoons balsamic vinegar, to taste

Fritter batter ingredients

1 cup flour
3 tablespoons unsweetened cocoa
2 tablespoons sugar
Pinch of salt
½ cup Champagne or dry white wine
2 large eggs
2 tablespoons milk
2 tablespoons melted butter

TO MAKE THE CHERRY SAUCE

Bring Port to a boil in a saucepan and add the cherries. Reduce the heat and let the cherries simmer until they are cooked and softened, but not falling apart. Remove the cherries from the liquid with a slotted spoon and set them aside. Taste the Port liquid for sweetness, add sugar if necessary, then reduce the Port over medium-high heat until it coats the back of a spoon. Remove the pan from the heat and return the cherries to the liquid. Add a touch of balsamic vinegar to brighten the sauce.

TO MAKE THE FRITTER BATTER

Mix the dry ingredients. Separately mix the wet ingredients.
Add the dry mixture to the wet mixture and blend until smooth.
Refrigerate for 2 hours.

TO MAKE THE TRUFFLES

Put the cream in a saucepan over medium heat and bring it just to a boil where tiny bubbles start coming to the surface. Remove the pan from the heat. Add the chocolate to the hot cream and stir until it melts and the mixture is smooth. Refrigerate until firm. Line a baking sheet with waxed paper. Scoop a scant tablespoon into a ball and put it on the waxed paper. A small ice cream scoop or melon baller will make life easier. You should have 24 truffles.

Put the baking sheet into the freezer for 20 minutes until the truffles solidify. Then roll the balls around on the waxed paper to smooth out the rough edges. Return them to the freezer for one hour. (If you want to make these ahead of time, put them in an airtight container in the freezer until you're ready to use them.)

TO MAKE THE FRITTERS

Heat 2–3 inches of vegetable oil in a pan to 375°. Drop several frozen truffles into the batter. Remove them from the batter with a fork or wooden skewer, allowing the excess batter to drip off. Drop the fritter into the oil (do this quite close to the surface so you don't splash yourself). Add several more truffles to the pan without crowding them. Fry for 2–3 minutes until the coating is crispy, making sure that you don't burn the chocolate batter.

TO SERVE

Place 3 fritters on 8 plates, place a spoonful of cherries to the side and then drizzle some of the cherry syrup around the fritters and fruit. Sprinkle with confectioners' sugar and serve with cherry sorbet.

"Nobody knows the truffles I've seen."

Truffle ingredients

¾ cup whipping cream

14 ounces bittersweet or semi-sweet chocolate, chopped

SCRAMBLED EGGS with LOBSTER, MASCARPONE, CAVIAR and SCALLOPS

For those times when you want to thank someone in the morning for a wonderful night before…this is the slowest way to make scrambled eggs – and creates the creamiest and most luxurious result. To set the tone and time the cooking, pour yourself a glass of Champagne and sip it leisurely as the eggs slowly set. Place the rest of the bottle in a silver ice bucket and share it with breakfast.

Serves 2

2 tablespoons butter

4 eggs, beaten

½ teaspoon salt

A few grindings of white pepper

3 ounces mascarpone

2 lobster tails

1 tablespoon butter

6 sea scallops

4 thick slices of bread or challah

1 ounce caviar, Osetra or your favorite

TO MAKE THE SCRAMBLED EGGS

Bring an inch or two of water to a boil in a medium saucepan and then turn the heat down so that the water gently simmers. Place a metal bowl over but not touching the simmering water. Add the butter to the bowl, and when it melts, swirl the bowl so that the butter coats the sides. Add the eggs, salt and pepper. Stir occasionally with a wooden spoon, and then more frequently as the eggs begin to cook and create soft curds – which will take 20 minutes or more.

While the eggs are cooking, steam the lobster tails over boiling water until the meat turns opaque, which will take 10 minutes or so, depending on the size of the tails. With kitchen shears, cut through the carapace on the underside of the tail (the non-red side) and pull out the meat. Cut it into generous 1-inch cubes.

As the eggs begin to thicken into tiny loose curds, stir the mascarpone to loosen it, and then stir it into the cooking eggs. Add the lobster meat and taste for seasoning. Add more salt and pepper as needed. Turn off the heat and let the bowl sit over the hot water so that the lobsters infuse the eggs with flavor as you cook the scallops and toast.

TO COOK THE SCALLOPS

Melt butter in a skillet over medium-high heat. Add the scallops and lower the heat to medium. When the underside develops a crust and is golden brown, turn and cook the other side.

TO MAKE THE TOAST POINTS

Place thick bread slices on a cookie sheet under the broiler until just golden. Flip the toast until the other side is done. Remove, cut off the crusts and slice on the diagonal.

TO SERVE

Spoon the eggs in a mound and top with a dollop of caviar. Serve with three scallops and two toast points on the side. Pour the perfectly chilled Champagne.

POACHED APPLES in CHOCOLATE GINGERBREAD COOKIE CUPS

We noticed a mysterious property when Shirlee was making the cookie cups for this recipe – they seem to disappear into thin air and there was a distinct staff outbreak of chocolate-ginger breath. I suggest doubling the recipe to make extra. Try them at Christmas (or your winter holiday of choice) filled with peppermint stick or eggnog ice cream and a little gingerbread man looking on.

Serves 6

Chocolate gingerbread cookie cup ingredients

½ cup brown sugar

3 tablespoons flour

½ teaspoon ginger

½ teaspoon cinnamon

½ teaspoon cloves

3 tablespoons quick-cooking oatmeal

2 tablespoons finely chopped almonds

1 tablespoon unsweetened cocoa

¼ teaspoon salt

2 tablespoons unsalted butter, melted

½ teaspoon vanilla extract

3 egg whites, lightly beaten

TO MAKE THE CHOCOLATE GINGERBREAD COOKIE CUPS

Spray 2 cookie sheets with vegetable oil or cover them with silicone sheets.

Mix the dry ingredients in a medium bowl. Combine the butter, vanilla and lightly beaten egg whites and then add them to the dry ingredients. Stir just until the dry ingredients are moistened.

Spoon 2 tablespoons of batter onto the cookie sheet and spread it into a 6-inch circle. You should be able to fit three cookies on a sheet. Bake at 350° for 10 minutes or until the edges seem dry.

Remove each cookie from the pan quickly and drape it over an inverted 8-ounce custard cup, a tapered juice glass, or whatever object will give you a shape that's pleasing. Mold the cookie around the cup or glass to form a cup shape. Let it cool completely before removing from the mold.

Poached apples

One of my favorite lists of ingredients – less than a full bottle of Champagne is required. Chill the remainder and place it in the cook.

Poached apple ingredients

¾ cup finely chopped crystallized ginger

2½ cups sugar

1½ cups apple juice or sparkling apple cider

3½ cups Champagne or dry white wine (if you want a little color, a dry rosé would add a pink tinge)

6 large apples, preferably Granny Smith, organic Golden Delicious or other firm, baking apple

Night owl instructions

Everything can be made the night before, but undercook the apples a bit. Keep the chocolate ginger cups in an airtight container so that they stay crisp. In the morning, heat up the syrup and add the apples to warm them.

TO POACH THE APPLES

Combine ginger, sugar and liquids and bring to a boil while you peel the apples and cut them into ¾-inch cubes. Reduce the heat so that the liquid is at a gentle boil then add the apple chunks. Poach the apples for 8–10 minutes depending on the firmness of the apple. They should be soft but still hold their shape. Remove the apple cubes from the liquid and set them aside. Return the liquid to a boil and reduce until it's syrupy.

TO SERVE

Place a Chocolate Ginger Cup in the center of each plate. Place a big scoop of ginger ice cream (see *Frozen Delights*, page 262 or substitute vanilla) in the cup, mound the poached apples next to the ice cream and garnish with a sprig of mint.

ROLLED RICOTTA OMELET with CHEESY POTATO CAKES

Serves 6

Ricotta filling ingredients

1 tablespoon butter

2 scallions, chopped

1 cup ricotta cheese

Salt and pepper to taste

Omelet ingredients

8 eggs, lightly beaten

½ teaspoon salt and freshly ground black pepper to taste

¼ cup freshly grated Romano cheese

1 teaspoon thyme

1 teaspoon oregano

Ingredients to assemble

½ cup fresh pesto sauce (see *Pantry*, page 276)

Chopped tomato to garnish

Wine suggestions
Cabernet Sauvignon; Cabernet Franc

TO MAKE THE RICOTTA FILLING

Melt the butter in a small skillet over medium heat and sauté the scallions until soft. To warm it, add the ricotta to the pan with the scallions. Set the pan aside in a warm area.

TO MAKE THE OMELETS

Combine all of the omelet ingredients in a mixing bowl and beat with a whisk.

Lightly coat the bottom of a medium skillet with olive oil and place it over medium-high heat. When the oil is hot but not smoking, add ¼ cup of the egg mixture or enough to make a thin pancake. Lower the heat and cook until the omelet is firm then flip it and cook briefly on the other side. Remove it from the pan and continue making the remaining omelets. (If you have two pans of the same size, start an omelet and when you flip the first one, start the next). Remove the finished omelet from the pan and spread it with the ricotta mixture, roll loosely and then keep it warm in a low oven (200°). Don't let the omelets sit too long or the scallions will add a nasty green tint to the eggs.

TO SERVE

Place one rolled omelet on a plate, spoon a generous helping of pesto over the omelet and then place two potato cakes next to it. Garnish with chopped tomato.

Alternatives: *Use a cilantro pesto and queso fresco mixed with the ricotta for a more Latin dish with fresh tomato salsa as a garnish. Or make a Ligurian pesto with walnuts and oregano (see Pantry, page 276).*

Cheesy potato cakes

Serves 6

1½ pounds unpeeled russet potatoes

1 to 4 tablespoons flour

1 egg

2 scallions, chopped and sautéed in butter until softened

1½ cups plus 2 tablespoons herbed bread crumbs, plus ¼ cup more for dredging

⅔ cup grated Parmesan, dry jack, asiago cheese or a combination of these or other favorite hard cheeses

Salt and pepper to taste

2 tablespoons olive oil for sautéing

Night owl instructions

The potato mixture can be prepared the day before, minimizing the addition of extra flour. Let the mixture come to room temperature before proceeding with the recipe.

TO PREPARE THE POTATO MIXTURE

Place the whole potatoes in boiling, salted water and boil until they're cooked but not mushy. Drain well in a colander for 10 minutes or so, then peel and mash them. Stir in a tablespoon of flour along with the egg, scallions, breadcrumbs and cheese until the mixture comes together. Let sit for 20 minutes. Add salt and pepper to taste. Add additional flour as needed if the mixture is too loose to hold together in patties.

TO COOK THE CAKES

Place a tablespoon of olive oil in a large sauté pan over medium-high heat. Form the potato mixture into silver dollar-sized patties using ⅓ cup of the potato mixture. Place ¼ cup breadcrumbs on a plate and lightly coat each patty on both sides. Turn the heat down to medium and place the patties into the pan. Sauté until the outside of the patty is crusty and brown on both sides.

Keep the patties warm in a low oven (200°) until ready to serve.

RASPBERRY SOUFFLÉ

It's so rewarding to deliver a soufflé to guests and be greeted by appreciative oohs and aahs. This version is very easy to prepare, and with no yolks, is cholesterol-free. Make the full recipe and, before baking, double-wrap any extra ramekins in plastic wrap and freeze them. On that day when you need a spectacular last minute treat, remove the plastic wrap and put the ramekins in the oven, still frozen, for 17 minutes and serve.

Serves 12

Raspberry syrup ingredients

6–8 ounces raspberries
2 tablespoons sugar
2 tablespoons water

Raspberry soufflé ingredients

2 cups sieved apricot jam, measured after sieving
2 tablespoons Chambord, Kirsch or other raspberry-flavored liqueur (Bonny Doon Winery makes a raspberry dessert wine that adds great flavor)
12 egg whites
Powdered sugar to garnish

Raspberry sauce ingredients

2 cups raspberries
¼ cup sugar
¼ cup water

Night owl instructions

Everything except baking can be done the night before. Cover the ramekins with plastic wrap and refrigerate them overnight. In the morning, make sure your guests are seated. Take the ramekins out of the refrigerator, remove the plastic wrap and place them in the preheated oven.

TO MAKE THE RASPBERRY SYRUP

Bring the raspberries, sugar and water slowly to a boil in a small saucepan. Strain out the seeds and let the mixture cool.

TO MAKE THE RASPBERRY SOUFFLÉ

Spray twelve 6-ounce soufflé dishes/ramekins with vegetable oil and dust with sugar. Place them on a baking sheet to make it easier to move them in and out of the oven.

Combine the raspberry syrup, sieved jam and liqueur in a large bowl.

Whisk the egg whites until they form peaks, in a copper bowl if you have one. Fold them into the jam mixture just until combined. Spoon into the prepared ramekins and level off the tops. (This may be done up to an hour ahead of baking. Keep refrigerated.)

Preheat oven to 375°.

Place the ramekins on the middle rack of a 350° oven and bake for 10–12 minutes. Don't peek before 10 minutes.

Remove, dust the soufflés quickly with powdered sugar and serve immediately with raspberry sauce.

TO MAKE THE RASPBERRY SAUCE

Combine ingredients in a saucepan and bring to a boil. Purée in a blender and strain through a fine sieve.

POPPERS FOR TWO

After the soufflé, two more surprises to start the year: muffins that come with their own cream cheese and jam, and poppers, eggs that look like holiday surprise packages. To complete the illusion, add a heatproof Cracker Jacks toy or secret message in a cellophane envelope to the eggs before rolling them in the filo.

Egg filling ingredients

2 teaspoons butter

1 teaspoon olive oil

3 scallions, chopped into ¼-inch pieces

1 serrano or jalapeño or Anaheim chile pepper, minced

5 eggs

2 tablespoons water

Salt and pepper to taste

3 tablespoons cream

Ingredients to assemble

6 sheets of filo, 9 x 13-inch

1 tablespoon melted butter

1 tablespoon olive oil

¼ cup grated Swiss or your favorite cheddar cheese

4 long chives (or substitute strips of the green part of a scallion) wilted in boiling water

Wine suggestions
Pinot Noir; Brut sparkling wine

Preheat oven to 350°.

TO PREPARE THE EGG FILLING

Melt butter and oil in a medium skillet over medium heat. Add scallions and chile pepper and sauté, stirring occasionally, until softened for 4–5 minutes.

Mix eggs, water and salt and pepper with a fork or an electric mixer. Pour into the skillet over the scallions. Leave them undisturbed until the bottom has begun to set. Loosen the bottom and stir (scramble) the eggs until they're still somewhat liquid, but nearly firm. Add the cream, stir and turn off the heat. They'll continue cooking as you prepare the filo.

TO ASSEMBLE

Mix the melted butter and oil. Place two filo sheets on your work surface. Brush each with the melted butter/oil mixture. Place another sheet on top of each and brush again. Add the final sheet and brush again. Add Swiss cheese to the scrambled eggs and stir. Place half of the scrambled egg mixture at the bottom of each filo stack, leaving a 1½-inch border. Roll the filo, encasing the eggs in the middle and leaving the edges free. Tie each end with a wilted chive so that it looks like a Christmas popper. Place the poppers on a baking sheet and bake at 350° for 15–20 minutes until golden brown.

CHEDDAR CHEESE SURPRISE MUFFINS

Makes 1 dozen

2 tablespoons sugar

2 tablespoons melted butter

2 tablespoons canola or other
   low-flavor oil

1 egg

1 cup milk

2 cups flour

1 tablespoon baking powder

¼ teaspoon garlic salt

a fresh grinding of white pepper

1 cup grated sharp cheddar cheese

8 ounces cream cheese,
   cut into 12 cubes

½ cup apricot or raspberry jam

Preheat oven to 400°.

In a mixing bowl, thoroughly blend the sugar, butter and oil. Add the egg and beat the mixture until fluffy and light-colored. Sift the dry ingredients together and add them to the mixing bowl alternately with the milk. Fold in the grated cheddar.

Butter a muffin tin, or spray it with oil, and half-fill each of the muffin cups with batter. Press a cube of cream cheese into each, and top with a spoonful of apricot jam. Cover with the remaining batter so no jam or cream cheese is visible. Bake for 12–15 minutes at 400° until the top bounces back when you press your finger on the surface.

Valentine's Day Decadence

Chocolate = Love

Roses and chocolate-chocolate

Rose petal sorbet
Chocolate-chocolate pancakes

———

I give you my heart

Chocolate banana ice cream heart with raspberry sorbet

———

Table for two

Chocolate fondue
Orange zest pound cake

———

Finale: the proposal

A chocolate box

ROSE PETAL SORBET

The trick to this sorbet is to let the floral flavor shine through without it tasting as though you're eating perfume. The secret, as with many a party, is to add Champagne, or "sparkling wine" as it's called outside of France. Add some to the sorbet and the rest to your glass.

Rose petal syrup ingredients
(makes 2 cups)

4 cups of petals from organically grown roses (the flavor is stronger in many red roses, and spicier in some like peach-colored Sonia)

1⅓ cups sugar

2 cups water

Sorbet ingredients

2 cups rose petal syrup

1 glass (¾ cup) of California Blanc de Blanc or Blanc de Noir sparkling wine from Domaine Carneros, Mumm, Domaine Chandon, Schramsberg, Iron Horse…

⅓ cup late harvest Riesling, Moscato, or Dolce if you're feeling indulgent

TO PREPARE THE ROSE PETAL SYRUP

Wash the petals and spin them dry in a salad spinner. Cut off and discard the yellowish-white tip at the base of the petals as it's a little bitter. Then chop the petals very finely.

Bring the water to a boil and add the sugar, stirring until it melts. Then add the petals and remove the pot from the heat. Cover it and let the mixture steep for at least 12 hours. Then strain and refrigerate the syrup until you're ready to use it.

TO MAKE THE SORBET

Combine all of the ingredients and freeze in an ice cream machine according to the manufacturer's instructions. Make the sorbet a day ahead if possible as it will have to harden further in the freezer before serving. Serve it nestled in a rose or float a scoop in Champagne.

CHOCOLATE-CHOCOLATE PANCAKES

As we prepared for the photography of this dish, Marc kept asking for more and more pancakes. He said a very tall stack would make a good photo. Then I realized the stack wasn't growing, he had completed the photography, and the pancakes were disappearing. There sat Marc, smeared with chocolate, smiling and chuckling like a kid caught with his hand in the cookie jar. Apparently sauce is optional.

Makes about 30 small pancakes

Pancake ingredients

1⅔ cups flour

⅓ cup unsweetened coca powder

2 teaspoons baking powder

¼ teaspoon salt

⅓ cup granulated sugar

1 cup chocolate chips

2 eggs

2 teaspoons vanilla

5 tablespoons butter, melted and cooled

1¼ cups (plus up to ¼ cup more) milk

Raspberry sauce ingredients

1 pint raspberries

2 tablespoons sugar

¼ cup water

¼ cup raspberry liqueur
    (or Grand Marnier or cognac)

Note: *If the griddle gets too hot, chocolate will burn. Keep the griddle just hot enough so that the batter barely sizzles when you pour it.*

TO MAKE THE PANCAKES

Put the flour, cocoa, baking powder, salt and sugar through a sieve placed over a large mixing bowl. Add the chocolate chips to the dry ingredients. Beat the eggs and vanilla together. Add melted butter, then milk and continue to blend. Pour the liquid mix over the dry ingredients and stir thoroughly. It should be about the consistency of a really good chocolate milkshake.

Place a platter in the oven and turn the heat to 200°. As you make the pancakes, put them on the platter so that they stay warm until you're ready to serve.

Place a griddle or a large skillet over moderate heat and brush the surface with a little melted butter. Using a ladle, drop batter onto the griddle to make pancakes about 2–3 inches across. Cook until the edges begin to look dry and bubbles appear on the surface. Flip gently and cook for another minute on the other side.

TO MAKE THE RASPBERRY SAUCE

Place half of the raspberries in a small saucepan over medium heat. Stir in the sugar, water and liqueur. When the raspberries start to collapse and liquefy, turn the heat down to low and cook until they're very soft. Pour through a strainer to remove the seeds, pushing against the solids to extract all of the juice. Add the remainder of the raspberries to the juice and stir. Set aside until the pancakes are done.

TO ASSEMBLE

Serve 3–5 pancakes per person, topped with the raspberry sauce and berries.

I give you my heart

CHOCOLATE-BANANA ICE CREAM HEART with RASPBERRY SORBET

These waffles start with a fluffy batter and become thin and slightly crispy when cooked, the better to stand up to the ice cream filling. They are best made as soon as the batter is prepared before the egg whites deflate. Should the object of your affection be late arriving at the breakfast table, keep the waffles warm in a 200° oven and spread the ice cream on when you see the whites of his eyes. (Or hers, of course.) One of our guests told me she fills the waffles and freezes them, serving them like ice cream sandwiches after they've thawed for 15 minutes or so. Ours never seem to make it to the freezer.

Makes 8 standard-sized waffles

4 eggs, separated
1 cup sour cream
¾ cup flour
⅓ cup cocoa powder
1 teaspoon baking soda
2 cups buttermilk
1 cup mashed bananas
   (usually 2 ripe ones)
5 tablespoons melted butter
2 cups chocolate mini chips

Ricotta ice cream (or substitute vanilla)
   as filling
Raspberry sorbet to garnish

Wine suggestions
Pinot Noir; Rosé sparkling wine

Special equipment: A waffle maker – preferably one with heart shapes.

Mix the egg yolks and sour cream in a mixing bowl. Stir in the flour, cocoa powder and baking soda. Mix in the buttermilk and bananas. Add the melted butter and chocolate chips and mix thoroughly. Beat the egg whites in a separate bowl until they form soft peaks when you lift the beaters out of the bowl. Fold ⅓ of the egg whites into the chocolate batter until well mixed. Then gently fold in the remaining whites.

Waffle makers vary, so follow the directions on yours. Make sure it's well heated to start, and brush with a little melted butter.

When the waffles are done, cut into hearts, squares or whatever shapes your machine creates, spread with ice cream and stack another waffle on top. Serve with raspberry sorbet.

CHOCOLATE FONDUE

There's something very intimate and primal about eating warm, gooey food out of the same pot. And sticky. And laughter-inducing. Not to mention the romance of eating by a fire, even if it's a teeny one…always a good way to start the day.

½ cup cream

8 ounces of bittersweet chocolate, chopped into small pieces

2 tablespoons cognac or brandy

Special equipment: A chocolate fondue pot, or use a ramekin set over a votive candle (like the type used to serve melted butter at a lobster bake) and small forks or skewers to spear the cake and fruit.

Bring the cream to a boil in a small saucepan. Pour it in a bowl over the chopped chocolate. Whisk until velvety smooth. Add the cognac and pour the mixture into the ramekin. Arrange the dipping choices on a fig leaf.

Dipping choices: Squares of orange zest pound cake (recipe follows), strawberries, large perfect raspberries or boysenberries, baby bananas, fresh fig halves, white nectarines, apricots… Let what's fresh in the market – and your imagination – be your guide.

Alternative: *For a spicy version, add ½ teaspoon of cayenne, ½ teaspoon of cinnamon and substitute tequila for the cognac. Serve with crispy flour tortilla and plantain chips.*

ORANGE ZEST POUND CAKE

Pound cake was traditionally made with a pound of flour, a pound of eggs, a pound of butter… This version is more of a half-a-pound cake. It's lighter, but still has that traditional dense texture that makes it hold together when dipped in a hot, thick chocolate fondue. Or cut a slice, top it with strawberries and whipped cream, and no one will miss the shortcake.

5 large eggs

1 tablespoon orange juice (see note)

1 teaspoon vanilla

2 teaspoons grated orange zest

2 sticks (8 ounces) unsalted butter at room temperature

1¾ cups sugar

½ teaspoon kosher salt

2 cups sifted cake flour

Preheat oven to 325°.

Lightly oil a 9 x 5-inch loaf pan and line the bottom with waxed paper or parchment.

Thoroughly whisk the eggs, juice, vanilla and grated orange zest together and set them aside.

In a mixer, whip the butter at high speed until it's smooth and light-colored. Add the sugar and salt and whip some more until the mixture is light and fluffy. At medium speed, slowly add the egg mixture. Beat for several more minutes until everything is fully incorporated. Then at low speed, add half the flour, then the remaining half, mixing well.

Pour the batter into the pan. Bake for 70 minutes until it's golden on top, springs back to a light touch, and a toothpick inserted in the middle comes out clean.

Put the hot pan on a rack and let it cool and settle for 15 minutes. Loosen the pound cake by sliding a knife around the rim and tip it out onto a rack. Remove the paper and let the cake cool completely before cutting.

Note: *To intensify the orange flavor, put ¼ cup of orange juice in a small saucepan and reduce it to a tablespoon over medium-high heat.*

A simple chocolate box to hold
a ring or a secret invitation,
the first step of a scavenger
hunt, a love note or a gift
certificate for a visit to Napa.

A CHOCOLATE BOX

This simple way to create a chocolate box came about when a darling and very nervous young man arrived at the Inn and told me he wanted to propose to his girlfriend. Having gotten her to Napa, he was at a loss as to how to proceed. She loved chocolate, so he was thinking of hiding the engagement ring in a cake and giving it to her at dinner that evening. With visions of broken teeth or at least chocolate encrusted diamonds, I volunteered to make him a box out of chocolate. That's when he told me he needed it in about half an hour.

The traditional method of constructing beautiful chocolate creations involves a finicky operation of "tempering" to get the chocolate to exactly the right temperature using double boilers, marble slabs and patience. If done wrong, which tends to happen when hurrying, the melted chocolate turns into a nasty grayish clump – not the impression you want to give when asking someone to share her life with you.

Instead, we created a box out of chocolate bars we had on hand. Apparently it produced the desired effect. They just returned to celebrate their 10th anniversary. And we placed a note of congratulatons in a chocolate box on the pillow.

contains 1 secret

6 small (1 or 1½-inch) chocolate bars, plus a couple of spares for experimentation

Note: *The are many choices for chocolate bars. Dean and Deluca, Hershey's, Scharffenberger and specialty chocolatiers like Bissinger's and Michel Richart make small chocolate bars that are individually wrapped or packaged as part of a tasting collection*

Heat a small skillet over medium heat. Melt one edge of a piece of chocolate by holding it against the warm skillet. Attach it to another piece of chocolate at a right angle, creating two sides of the box in an "L" shape. Stand this section on your work surface to cool and harden. Repeat with two more sides.

One side of each section will be a little longer than the other by the width of the piece of chocolate and because you've melted part of one of the pieces. To assure your box will have square corners, before melting any more edges, place the two sections together to determine the way they'll fit best. Then melt the two outer edges of one of the sections and adhere it to the other section. You now have a bottomless and topless box.

After this has cooled, take another piece of chocolate and briefly melt all four edges. Place this in the bottom of the box and let it harden in place.

If you have any sloppy looking seams, heat a knife in boiling water or over a flame and smooth the edges with the warm knife.

Put your secret in the box, place another piece of chocolate on top, and tie with a beautiful ribbon. The next step is up to you.

Original Sin

another chocolatey poem by tony

They say we're patterned in our mortal souls,
With "original" sin from days of old,
From Adam and Eve so the story goes,
Comes a spiritual crack from our head to our toes.

But not for me, you see, is the old "apple" story,
If I am going to be flawed, let me be flawed by glory!
Make decadent chocolate MY original sin,
This makes good sense…given the shape I'm in!

To begin…I'm not sure I want absolution,
From priest or pastor or religious institution,
I think I can live with my chosen sin,
Decadent chocolate…where to begin?

First of all, it's something I can turn to at night,
When bothering God…just doesn't seem right,
If all I've got is a little sinful craving,
I lunge for that bonbon which I have been saving.

And for days when I can tolerate a little more guilt,
Hershey's Kisses in my mouth I do love to melt,
Yes, they're a few extra calories which I do not need.
But the guilt's also manageable…don't you agree?

And for BIG guilt there's that slab of chocolate cake,
When no one is looking…a double serving I take,
That guilt hits me solidly right out of the gate
But the cake is intoxicating, and I just can't wait!

Chocolate is always there for me…like original sin,
In wrappers, chocolate hearts and tight little tins,
It saves me from sins of a more mortal kind,
Which are expensive or illegal or which my wife minds!

So on my tombstone let there be just one line:
"He Wasn't A Sinful Man…But Chocolate…
He Liked That Just Fine!"

Vernal Equinox: Spring Anticipation

Spring time is chocolate time!

Winter's almost gone

Blood orange soup with chocolate Madeleine spoons

Eggs in a nest

———

Spring has sprung

Chocolate strawberry shortcake

Parmesan crêpes with asparagus and wild mushrooms

CHOCOLATE MADELEINE SPOONS

For anyone who's ever had a huge craving for chocolate while dieting, this is the answer. You really can eat just one bite.

Makes 12–15 spoonfuls

1 egg
2 tablespoons sugar
1 tablespoon unsalted butter, melted
2 tablespoons flour
½ teaspoon baking powder
1 tablespoon cocoa powder
Powdered sugar for sprinkling

Preheat the oven to 350°.

Beat the egg with the sugar. Mix in the melted butter. Put the flour, baking powder and cocoa powder through a sieve and fold into the egg mixture. Fill buttered teaspoons or tablespoons ⅔ full and place on a cookie sheet, propping the spoon handles on the edge so that the batter doesn't fall out. Bake for 5 minutes, or a minute or two longer if using a larger spoon. Sprinkle with powdered sugar.

BLOOD ORANGE SOUP

The first time I saw a blood orange was in Italy at Villa d'Este on Lake Como in 1985. John asked for orange juice at breakfast and they brought what we thought was tomato juice. When our Italian and the waiter's English were unequal to the task, he brought an orange, cut it open, and showed us the source. Slightly less acidic and fragrant with memories, blood oranges are my first choice when they're available. In California, they begin to ripen in January and last until the first strawberries appear in the spring.

Serves 8

1½ pounds blood oranges, peeled, sectioned and seeded
⅓ cup sugar
½ vanilla bean
2 cups blood orange juice
2 cups mandarin or other orange juice

Place orange sections in a heavy sauté pan. With a sharp knife, scrape the seeds from the vanilla bean and add it and the scrapings to the pan along with the sugar. Place over a medium-high flame and cook until the sugar melts and the mixture starts to bubble – 4 or 5 minutes. Reduce heat and cook for about 10 more minutes so that the blood orange sections are soft but still intact. Add the juice and just warm it slightly. Serve with a chocolate spoon cookie.

TO SECTION AN ORANGE

This is the citrus version of boning and skinning a chicken. The goal is to remove the skin and underlying white pith, any seeds and the membrane between the sections of the orange.

At the top and bottom of the orange, slice off the peel and pith and set the orange on your cutting board. Following the curve of the orange with your knife, slice away the remaining peel and pith.

Blood orange sections are typically smaller than those of other oranges, and the membrane is more delicate. If the membrane is so delicate that it's almost indistinguishable from the orange section, then forget about getting rid of it and cut the peeled blood orange in slices across the equator.

If, however, the membrane behaves itself and stays intact, then it's strong enough to be annoying in the soup, and also strong enough to cut away. Over a bowl to catch the juice, hold the orange in your hand and cut as close to the membrane between two sections as you can get, stopping when you reach the middle of the orange. Twist your knife so that the blade travels up the opposite side of the section to pry it away from the membrane on the other side. Repeat until all of the sections are removed.

EGGS in a NEST

Special equipment: For the hollandaise, a blender or food processor – use an immersion blender if you have one as it makes it easy to see how the sauce is thickening. For the nests, a cookie sheet covered with a silicone (Silpat) pad.

Hollandaise sauce ingredients

3 egg yolks

Juice from ½ lemon

½ teaspoon salt

¼ teaspoon cayenne

1 stick (¼ pound) unsalted butter

A dash of paprika to garnish

Nest ingredients

2 cups grated dry cheese (Parmesan, pecorino, asiago or aged jack cheese)

Poached egg ingredients

8 whole eggs

TO MAKE THE HOLLANDAISE SAUCE

Put everything except the butter in the blender. Melt a stick of butter until it's bubbly, but before it turns brown. Let the bubbles subside. Start the blender, then slowly drizzle in the melted butter, still blending, until the mixture emulsifies and reaches the consistency of mayonnaise. If it gets too thick, add a teaspoon or so of sour cream until the consistency is right. The hollandaise can be kept warm by putting the container in a bowl of warm water.

TO PREPARE THE NESTS

Preheat oven to 400°. Line a cookie sheet with a silicone (Silpat) sheet to prevent the cheese from sticking. (If you don't have one, grease the cookie sheet with a little spray of cooking oil.) Sprinkle the cheese into four 6-inch lacy circles on the sheet. Place the cookie sheet in the preheated oven and let the cheese melt until bubbly and slightly brown – about 10 minutes. When it starts to brown slightly, lift each circle out quickly with a spatula and drape it over a small bowl. As it cools, it will harden into whatever shape you leave it in, so work fast.

TO POACH THE EGGS

Over high heat, bring 3 inches of water to a boil in a medium saucepan and then turn the heat down until the water is just simmering with steam coming off the top and a tiny bubble or two appearing every few seconds. Crack an egg into a small bowl and pour it gently into the simmering water. Repeat with the other eggs. Place them in the water in a clockwise circle to make it easier to remember in which order they'll be done. Cook until the white is firm and the yolk is still runny. Remove with a slotted spoon.

Sautéed shiitake ingredients

1 tablespoon butter

1 tablespoon olive oil

¼ cup finely chopped scallions (a.k.a. green onions)

½ pound cleaned, de-stemmed and sliced shiitake mushrooms, or substitute portabellos or crimini

Salt and pepper to taste

Salad ingredients

4 cups of baby greens – mesclun, spinach or arugula

½ cup aioli (see *Pantry*, page 269) or make a simple three to one oil and vinegar dressing

TO SAUTÉ THE SHIITAKE

Melt the butter in a medium-sized skillet over medium heat. Toss in the chopped scallions and let them cook for 3–4 minutes, turning with a wooden spoon. Once they're a bit wilted, add the sliced shiitakes. Toss them with the butter and scallions and cook until they turn soft and the texture changes from stiff and dry to moist and flexible. Taste one. If it has a meaty character, it's done. Sprinkle with a little salt and a few turns of freshly ground pepper.

TO ASSEMBLE

Dress the greens with the aioli and put a handful on the plate. Place a nest partially on the salad. Put a couple of heaped spoonfuls of sautéed mushrooms in each nest. Top with 2 poached eggs. Nap with hollandaise. Sprinkle a little paprika on top and serve.

Optional: Place a warmed slice of Canadian bacon or parma ham under the eggs, or grilled asparagus spears, parboiled broccoli florets… The only limit is your imagination and what's available in the market.

Troubleshooting poached eggs: If the egg white spreads out in the water into ghostly white strands and just sits there, the water isn't quite hot enough. You can try turning the egg over, using a wooden spoon, to get it back together, or consider this the sacrificial egg and feed it to the dog while you wait for the heat to come up again.

If the egg starts to scramble and cooked bits of yolk rise to the top, the water is probably boiling madly. Turn it down.

If, no matter what you do, the whites and yolks separate, your eggs may not be especially fresh. Poached eggs hold together best with recently laid eggs. Try slipping the whole egg, in the shell, into the simmering water for 90 seconds. Then crack the egg and continue. This procedure can help keep the egg from separating.

Another tip is to put a rubber band around the carton of eggs the night before and store the box on its side in the refrigerator. The yolks will stay in the center of the eggs rather than settling towards the heavier bottom end.

If you want to cook the eggs ahead of time, place the poached eggs in a bowl of cool water. When it's time to serve, put them back into the simmering water to heat.

CHOCOLATE STRAWBERRY SHORTCAKE

When the "strawberry lady" on the Silverado Trail opens for business, there's a frisson of excitement among locals as the word spreads, because there are strawberries and then there are STRAWBERRIES. No white shoulders or hollow centers here. The berries are grown for local consumption, not shipping, so are picked when ripe. With courage, if you wait one more day, risking letting them go too far, the flavors are so intense that the aroma wafts out of the kitchen, down the driveway and stops traffic on Oak Knoll Avenue. Well, it would if we didn't eat them right away, or turn them into sorbet, or serve them with these dark, double-chocolate shortcakes, or all of the above.

Serves 8

Shortcake ingredients

1¾ cups flour
⅓ cup cocoa powder
½ cup confectioner's sugar
2½ teaspoons baking powder
1 teaspoon salt

6 tablespoons cold unsalted butter,
**   cut into chunks**
2 large eggs
½ cup heavy cream
2 teaspoons vanilla
½ cup chocolate chips

Filling/topping ingredients

2 pints strawberries, sliced
1 cup heavy cream, whipped with
**   2 tablespoons of powdered sugar**
**   and a splash of Grand Marnier.**
1 pint strawberry sorbet

Place the dry ingredients in a food processor and blend. Add the butter and cut in just until blended. Mix together the eggs, cream and vanilla and add all at once. Blend, then add chocolate chips. Shape the dough into an 8-inch disk, place on a cookie sheet, cover loosely with waxed paper and chill in the refrigerator for at least half an hour.

Preheat oven to 375°.

Place the chilled dough on a work surface and cut it like a pie into 8 wedges. Separate and place them on a greased cookie sheet and bake for 22 minutes. Cool slightly and slice the top half off.

Fill with sliced strawberries, whipped cream and serve with strawberry sorbet, garnished with a mint sprig.

"All you need is love. But a little chocolate now and then doesn't hurt."
Charles M. Schulz

PARMESAN CRÊPES with ASPARAGUS and WILD MUSHROOMS

Asparagus, that traditional harbinger of spring, is a sure sign that the garden is beginning its annual transformation. They grow well from Maine to California and are available at farmers markets nationwide at the same time as the first spring shiitake, and, if you're lucky, the meaty and intensely flavorful porcini, a.k.a. *cep* or *cêpe* to the French. The sensuous combination of earthy mushrooms with the vibrant crunch of asparagus and piquant, slightly salty Parmesan creates layers of flavor to awaken your palate to a new season of taste delights.

Makes 12

Crêpes ingredients

3 eggs

1 cup cold milk

½ cup Champagne (if you don't want to use Champagne, increase the amount of milk by ½ cup)

3 tablespoons brandy or cognac

1 cup flour

½ cup grated Parmesan or aged Sonoma Dry Jack cheese

6 tablespoons butter, melted

20 chives, sliced in half lengthwise, optional

2 to 3 tablespoons cooking oil and a pastry brush

PARMESAN CRÊPES

To produce exceptionally tender crêpes, make the batter at least 2 hours before it is to be used and refrigerate it. As the batter chills, the flour expands and absorbs the liquid and the gluten in the flour gets a chance to rest.

TO MAKE THE CRÊPE BATTER

Place the eggs in a mixing bowl. Either by hand or with an electric mixer, whisk the eggs and then whisk in the milk, bubbly and cognac. To avoid lumps, sprinkle the flour over the surface and whisk it into the liquids. Add the cheese and melted butter, then whisk the batter vigorously for 4–5 minutes so everything is thoroughly incorporated. It should be the consistency of thick cream. Cover the batter and refrigerate it for at least 2 hours or overnight.

TO PREPARE THE CRÊPES

The first is the sacrificial crêpe to test the consistency of your batter, the exact amount you need for the pan, and the heat. If the crêpes are thicker than you'd like, thin the batter with additional milk, gently whisking in a tablespoon at a time. Once you get used to the procedure, to save time you can keep two pans going at once.

Brush a 7 or 8-inch skillet or crêpe pan lightly with oil and heat it over medium-high heat until the pan is hot but not smoking.

Pour about ¼ cup of batter into the middle of the skillet and rotate it so the batter covers the bottom of the pan in a thin layer. Quickly lay 4 chive pieces in stripes across the surface. Cook the crêpe until the bottom is light brown, 1–2 minutes. Turn it over with a spatula, or by a toss of the pan, and cook until it is lightly browned on the other side, about 30 seconds. Slide the crêpe onto a rack or dry work surface and let it cool for several minutes before stacking it on a plate. This keeps the crêpes from sticking together.

Continue until all of the batter is used.

Crêpes may be kept warm by covering them with a dish and placing them in a low 200° oven.

WILD MUSHROOM FILLING

Clean the mushrooms with a mushroom brush or damp towel. If they're very dirty, place them in a colander and rinse with cold water. This is usually not done because mushrooms quickly absorb water, but as they're going to be in a sauce with broth, a little extra water won't hurt.

Heat the oil in a large saucepan over medium heat. Add the onion, garlic and parsley. Cook, stirring, until the onions begin to color and soften, 4–5 minutes.

Add the fresh, cleaned mushrooms. Raise the heat to medium-high and cook for 4–5 minutes, stirring a few times. Add the wine. Cook and stir until the wine is almost all reduced.

Season with salt and a few grindings of black pepper. Add the broth and bring the mixture to a boil, then lower the heat and simmer, uncovered, for 20–30 minutes. Taste and adjust the seasonings. Stir the Parmesan into the sauce.

Filling ingredients

2 pounds assorted wild mushrooms, sliced (shiitake, oyster, porcini, crimini…)

2 tablespoons olive oil

1 small onion, finely minced

2 garlic cloves, finely minced

¼ cup finely chopped flat leaf parsley

1 cup dry white wine (Chardonnay, Viognier, Chenin Blanc…)

1½ cups homemade chicken or beef broth (or substitute low-sodium canned)

½ teaspoon salt

Freshly ground pepper

½ cup freshly grated Parmesan or aged Sonoma Dry Jack cheese

TO ASSEMBLE

Break off and discard the woody bottom of each asparagus spear – they'll snap where the tender part begins. Trim the edge with a sharp knife.

To blanch the asparagus, bring 2 inches of salted water to a boil in a large saucepan. Add the asparagus and cook until it turns bright green and softens, but before it gets mushy and khaki colored. For skinny asparagus, this will take only 2–3 minutes. For thick spears, 4–5 minutes will do it.

Place a crêpe, chive-side down, on your work surface. Put two asparagus spears in the middle of the crepe. With a slotted spoon, place mushrooms on top of the asparagus and fold the edges of the crepe over. Serve two per person, seam-side down on the plate. Garnish with the extra sauce that's left in the pan after you've spooned out the mushrooms and sprinkle additional Parmesan cheese on top.

Ingredients to assemble

24 asparagus spears

12 Parmesan crêpes

Wild mushrooms in sauce

½ cup grated Parmesan cheese

Night owl instructions

Crêpes can be made the night before, or even days before as they freeze perfectly if well wrapped. Double the recipe and make enough for two meals.

In the morning, warm the crêpes by putting them on a plate, covering them with another plate or aluminum foil, and placing them in a warm (200°) oven while you get the rest of the meal ready.

The mushroom filling can be prepared the night before and then reheated. Asparagus stays crisp if prepared just before serving, so I don't recommend blanching them ahead of time.

Alternative

Place a thin slice of soft creamy cheese like Bellwether Crescenza or a runny teleme on top of the asparagus. Fold and place the crêpes in a baking pan, cover with foil and bake in a 350° oven for 10 minutes to melt the cheese.

4th of July
Picnic Brunch
And let the fireworks begin

Chocolate egg cream

Star-spangled cobbler

Light up your mouth devilish eggs

Firecracker sausage bundles

Watermelon ice pops

Eggs and bakin' – lemon "eggs" and streaky chocolate bakin' strips

Red, white and blueberry muffins

CHOCOLATE EGG CREAM

An old-fashioned New York City soda fountain drink, a traditional egg cream contains neither egg nor cream. But if you add a scoop of ice cream, it does become an ice cream soda, so there is *some* descriptive truth to be found in New York. And while we're on that subject, don't ever try to order a New York Steak in New York – it's called a shell steak in the City. And if someone asks if you want "regular coffee", don't be surprised when it arrives with lots of cream and two sugars already added. New Yorkers revel in their idiosyncrasies. But as someone who insists on serving chocolate for breakfast, who am I to talk?

In researching this recipe, I spoke to my friend Gene Daly, source for all things New York. Horrified at the idea that I would consider using anything else, he insists it's not a proper egg cream unless it's made with Fox's U Bet chocolate syrup, found in the kosher food section of large supermarkets.

Egg cream ingredients (for each)

- **2 tablespoons chocolate syrup – your own, Fox's U Bet, or other favorite store-bought**
- **2 tablespoons milk (traditional), half-and- half (better) or cream (my favorite)**
- **Seltzer water to fill the glass**

Chocolate syrup ingredients

- **⅓ cup cocoa powder**
- **½ cup sugar**
- **⅓ cup hot water**

Chocolate syrup

Chocolate syrup is always handy to have in the refrigerator for emergencies – like heeding an emergency call for an egg cream or ice cream soda. It can also be added to fresh yogurt with some crunchy bran cereal on top to take the edge off of all that healthiness.

Mix chocolate syrup and milk in the bottom of a tall soda fountain glass. Add seltzer and a straw. Drink while the bubbles still tickle your nose.

Note: *Seltzer water is available in cans if you don't have the traditional bottle with a charger – although those are much more fun and come in handy when acting out the parts in old Three Stooges movies.*

TO MAKE THE CHOCOLATE SYRUP

Mix the cocoa and sugar in a small bowl or pyrex cup. Add half of the hot water and stir until the sugar and cocoa powder are dissolved. Add the remaining water and stir until smooth. Keep in the refrigerator until needed.

STAR-SPANGLED COBBLER

Summer berries are so accommodating. They arrive in patriotic colors and ripen in time for the 4th of July. They are also juicy when baked, so let the cobbler cool before trying to transport it to your picnic site or everything it touches will be colored holiday-appropriate.

Serves 8–12

Cheddar pastry ingredients

1 cup flour

¼ teaspoon salt

⅓ cup butter or shortening

½ cup shredded cheddar cheese

1 or 2 tablespoons ice water

Fruit filling ingredients

3 pints strawberries, hulled and halved

1 pint blackberries or blueberries

½ cup sugar

¼ cup flour

Juice from 1 lemon

½ teaspoon ground cinnamon

½ teaspoon freshly ground nutmeg

2 tablespoons butter, cut into ¼-inch cubes

TO MAKE THE PASTRY

Combine the dry ingredients and cut in the butter or shortening with a pastry blender (or whiz in a food processor) until the mixture looks thoroughly blended. Stir in the cheese. Sprinkle one tablespoon of ice water evenly over the pastry. Stir with a fork and shape into a ball. If it won't shape into a ball, add another tablespoon of water. To make it easier to roll out, wrap the ball of dough in waxed paper or a plastic bag and put it into the refrigerator to chill while you assemble the fruit.

TO ASSEMBLE THE COBBLER

In a lightly buttered 10 x 6 x 2-inch baking dish, arrange the berries in a flag shape with the blackberries holding forth in the upper left corner and the strawberries in the rest. Sprinkle with lemon juice. Mix together the dry ingredients and sprinkle the mixture over the berries. Cut the butter into tiny pieces and sprinkle them over the top.

On a lightly floured surface, roll out the cheddar pastry to ⅛-inch thickness. With a star-shaped cookie cutter, cut out 6 stars along one edge. With a knife, slice the remaining dough into six ½-inch strips. Arrange in a flag pattern over the berries.

Bake at 350° for 35 minutes until the crust is golden and the berries are bubbly and tender.

Alternatives: *When figs are in season, substitute them for the berries and create a lattice pattern with the cheddar crust. Apples are another good choice, and you can substitute asiago cheese for the cheddar. When pears are available, sprinkle with chopped walnuts and use a blue cheese in the topping for a classic French combination.*

LIGHT UP YOUR MOUTH DEVILISH EGGS

This is the time to use the eggs that have been in the refrigerator the longest. They're the easiest to peel. If you plan to make the devilish eggs immediately, pour off the hot water when the eggs are done and shake them around in the pan to crack the shells. Cover with cold water and then peel.

Makes 1 dozen

6 eggs

1 tablespoon Champagne vinegar (or white vinegar)

1 small jalapeño pepper

2 tablespoons minced onion or shallot

¼ teaspoon cayenne pepper

1 tablespoon jalapeño mustard (see *Pantry*, page 272) or substitute Dijon mustard

2 tablespoons sour cream

2 tablespoons aioli (see *Pantry*, page 269) or substitute mayonnaise

½ teaspoon salt, or to taste

Paprika and chopped chives

Cover eggs with water in a saucepan and place a lid on the pan. Bring to a boil over medium-high heat. Remove the pan from the heat and let it stand for 10 minutes. Remove the eggs, rinse them with cold water and refrigerate until they're chilled. Peel the eggs and cut them in half the long way. Remove the yolks and place them in a bowl and mash with a fork. Mix in the rest of the ingredients. Refill the whites with the mixture and garnish with paprika and chopped chives.

FIRECRACKER
SAUSAGE BUNDLES

While hot dogs may be traditional fare on the 4th of July, sausage makers like Bruce Aidells have launched a trend of alternatives made with chicken and other identifiable ingredients. Because you know what they say about the hot dog – its ingredients are best kept secret. That said, there are also some great hot dog makers – in Napa we have Long Meadow Ranch, using organically raised grass-fed beef, Hobbs for pork and several local butchers who make their own. Farmers' markets and your regional organic produce directory can provide names of your local purveyors. For picnics, choose sausages that taste good at picnic-temperature, unless you're planning to barbecue on-site. Chicken-apple, chicken-mango and habañero chicken are all popular alternatives.

TO PREPARE

Grill a variety of pre-cooked sausages, wrap them in a bundle, tie with scallion, leek green or festive ribbon and serve with 5-chile ketchup and jalapeño mustard (see *Pantry*, page 272). For a festive start to your picnic, ignite sparklers in the middle of the bundle and lead the way to the picnic blanket.

WATERMELON ICE POPS

On a hot day, grown-ups are the first to grab these pops, racing children to the stash, so make plenty. Prepare them the day before to assure they're frozen hard, and pack at the last minute in a separate cooler with ice packs.

Makes 8 small pops

2 cups watermelon, seeds and rind removed

½ cup superfine sugar

Juice from one lime

½ teaspoon salt

Special equipment: Pop molds, or use small Dixie cups. Pop sticks are available at gourmet shops or medical supply houses.

Blend all of the ingredients in a food processor or blender until the sugar dissolves. Pour into pop molds and freeze.

EGGS AND BAKIN' – LEMON "EGGS" and STREAKY CHOCOLATE BAKIN' STRIPS

When guests arrive, we ask about food allergies or aversions so we can tailor breakfast to their likes and desires. I expected the occasional allergy to strawberries or reluctance to eat onions, but a new one to me was "eggs that look like eggs." Who knew? Apparently the sight of a yolk first thing in the morning is the last thing they want to see. These lemon "eggs" were created to help break through that phobia. And with soft eggs, of course there must be bakin'.

Lemon "eggs" ingredients (1 dozen)

¾ cup sugar
¼ cup cornstarch
2½ cups whole milk
3 egg yolks
Pinch of salt
2 tablespoons lemon zest
½ cup lemon juice
2 tablespoons butter, at room temperature
6 kumquats, ends removed to create 12 "yolks"

Streaky bakin' ingredients (16 rashers)

¾ cup butter, softened (1½ sticks)
6 talespoons powdered sugar
Grated zest of an orange
1 tablespoon orange juice
2¼ cups flour

1 ounce melted dark chocolate, plus a little extra for assembling
1 beaten egg white

TO MAKE THE LEMON "EGGS"

Special equipment: 12 small egg cups.

Mix the sugar and cornstarch in a saucepan and whisk in the milk and yolks. Add the zest and salt. Place over medium heat, whisking until it thickens. Remove the pan from the heat and stir in the lemon juice and butter. Strain through a sieve into a pitcher to make it easier to pour into egg cups. Mound and round the top so that it resembles an egg. Top each with a piece cut off the end of a kumquat.

TO MAKE THE STREAKY BAKIN'

The less professional and perfect these cookies look, the more they resemble bacon, so don't fuss with getting all of the slices exactly straight or the edges tidy.

Preheat oven to 350°.

Beat the butter and sugar until smooth. Mix in the orange zest, juice and flour. Divide the dough in half and add the melted chocolate to one portion.

Roll out the white dough into a rectangle 3 inches wide and ¼ inch thick. Repeat with the chocolate dough. Brush the egg white over the white dough and top it with the chocolate. Gently run a rolling pin over the stack so they stick together.

Cut the rectangular stack in half, the short way. Brush one half with egg white and drizzle on the extra melted chocolate. Place the other half on top. You now have four layers. Slice through the layers to make ¼-inch-thick cookies. Scatter any crumbs on top and press them into the cookies. Place the cookies on a greased or Silpat-coated cookie sheet and bake for 10 minutes at 350°.

RED, WHITE and BLUEBERRY MUFFINS

By the time you finish the last chorus of the Star-Spangled Banner (or God Save the Queen or La Marseillaise, for that matter), these muffins will be ready to go into the oven. Everything is mixed in one bowl and sifting is optional. The one important thing to remember is to preheat the oven. If it isn't at full temperature when the pans go in, your muffins won't get that nice high dome.

Makes 12 standard muffins and
12 mini-muffettes

1 cup sugar

⅓ cup oil

2 eggs

1 cup half-and-half (or milk, if you insist, but then increase oil to ½ cup)

4 teaspoons baking powder

1 teaspoon salt

3 cups flour

1 cup dried cranberries or cherries

1½ cups large, perfect blueberries (discard any soft or broken berries as the texture won't work in the muffins and they'll stain the batter)

⅓ cup brown sugar to sprinkle over the tops

Preheat oven to 400°.

TO MAKE THE BATTER

Mix the sugar and oil until they're completely blended. Add the eggs alternately with the half-and-half, beating after each addition. Then add the baking powder and salt and beat them in thoroughly. Mix in the flour and the dried fruit. Gently fold in the blueberries.

TO BAKE

Spoon the batter into greased muffin tins, filling the cups two-thirds of the way. Sprinkle tops with brown sugar. Bake in a very well preheated oven at 400° for 15–18 minutes until the tops spring back when lightly tapped.

Recipe for a
perfect night's sleep

*...and now I lay me
down to eat*

Mostly chocolate chip cookies

How to make a bed

MOSTLY CHOCOLATE CHIP COOKIES

David Jackson (formerly of La Residence Country Inn in Napa) deserves the credit (or blame) for our finding Oak Knoll Inn in 1992, and is the person I've turned to for help too many times to count. In addition to his skills in restarting water systems in the middle of the night, laying marble (ditto), and fixing just about anything that can go wrong, he makes superb chocolate chip cookies. I begged for the recipe, as they're perfect to eat in bed. Or for dessert. Or as a snack. Or standing on your head, for that matter. And if you're only going to have one cookie (like that's going to happen) shouldn't it be huge?

Makes 18 huge cookies

½ pound butter (2 sticks), softened

1 cup brown sugar

1 cup granulated sugar

2 eggs

1 teaspoon baking soda

1 teaspoon salt

1 tablespoon vanilla

2¼ cups flour

10 ounces Guittard Super
  Cookie Chips

11 ounces milk chocolate chips

12 ounces semi-sweet chocolate chips

1½ cups chopped walnuts

Note: *The various chocolate chips happen to come in differently sized bags. Feel free to substitute, but only the best. Recently I've discovered See's chocolate chips, which are addictive.*

Preheat oven to 375°.

Cream the butter, sugar and eggs in a mixing bowl. Then add the baking soda, salt and vanilla. Mix in the flour and then add the chips and nuts.

Using a medium-sized ice cream scoop, place balls of dough on a greased baking sheet, flatten each slightly with your palm and leave space between cookies for them to expand.

Bake for 18–19 minutes. Try to share.

HOW TO MAKE A BED

One of our most frequently requested recipes, how to make a bed, like most good concoctions, depends heavily on great ingredients. One of our guiding philosophies at the Oak Knoll Inn is that eating and sleeping are among the only things in life that we have to do, and we should do them very well.

1 firm mattress

1 featherbed

1 hypoallergenic cotton featherbed cover

1 deep-sided pillowtop mattress pad

1 fitted bottom sheet, with at least 15-inch sides

1 down duvet

1 hypoallergenic duvet cover

1 sheet material duvet cover

2 down king-size pillows per person, one full-, one medium-weight

2 king-size hypoallergenic pillow covers

2 king-size pillowslips

Note: There is no such thing as no-iron sheets. The scent and feel of freshly laundered and ironed sheets next to your skin is luxuriously soothing and begins to calm the day's cares as your cheek hits the pillow. We wash the duvet covers, sheets and pillowcases in Arm & Hammer "Free" detergent, which has no dyes or aromas, and then iron them. If you don't like to iron, a quality laundry will do it for you.

SHOPPING

This is a very sensuous experience, so do it in person, not over the Internet or through a catalog. Shop where you know there are wonderful linens and they'll let you open all of the packages or will have samples available.

Mattress: Get the top of the line. You'll probably have your mattress and bed linens for years, will use them daily, and, of course, you deserve the best. A firm, best quality mattress will provide support for your back and bones, and will be softened next to your skin by what we're adding next.

Featherbed: Squeeze it. It should feel soft and compact, without any obvious feathers. If it's been packed in a zippered bag, as many of them are, it should burst out when you unzip it because it's so anxious to get back into its desired shape. The outside material should be high-density cotton. Test several. The ones with less desirable materials will be noisy when you touch and squeeze them. Get feathers, not down. Down sounds good but it will compress and flatten.

Featherbed cover: Get a hypoallergenic cover of high-density cotton. Allergists have told us that people with "down" allergies are actually allergic to feathers, and more accurately, to the bits and pieces that come with feathers – somewhat like the dander on dogs and cats is to those with animal allergies. Even if you don't have allergies, this cover will protect the featherbed from acquiring dust and other environmental additives (like cat fur, for those of us who sleep with critters).

Mattress pad: The mattress pad will protect and secure the featherbed in place, so get one with deep elastic sides and a pillow top for even more softness under your skin. Once again, feel it and wrinkle it. If it's noisy, keep looking.

Sheets, duvet cover and pillow slips: Cotton percale, long-staple cotton, often from Egypt, Portugal or Italy, is best. Thread count is important, but after 350 threads per inch, it becomes less critical than the quality of the cotton. Percale is smooth and will maintain a wonderful texture, whereas "sateen" and other pretenders will start to "pill" after wear and washing. Frette make high-quality linens for the hospitality trade and have started making their sheets available to the public (see *Resources*).

Duvet: Look for high-quality down, with a dense cotton cover and baffles to keep the down from shifting and settling in one end or the other. The baffles should create channels or boxes, but the top shouldn't be sewn directly to the bottom or there will be cold spots. The weight of the duvet depends on your climate and whether you like to snuggle under covers or have something light on top of you. We use two weights – a light one for summer and heavier one for winter. If you're concerned about allergies, get a zippered hypoallergenic cover, like the one for the featherbed above.

King-size pillows: In addition to supporting your tired head for a good night's sleep, king-size pillows can be stacked for reading in bed and don't get hot as quickly as standard-sized pillows. Get one pillow that's softer than the other so it can be smooshed into the perfect shape to support your back or sore knee. Good quality down pillows are pricey, but oh so worth it!

Pillow protector: One piece of fabric away from your face, the protector should be soft, smooth, 100% cotton, and quiet. If you like a medium to firm pillow, a quilted, faceted protector provides extra support.

TO ASSEMBLE

Starting from the bottom up, on top of your firm mattress, place the featherbed, which is inside a zippered all-cotton hypoallergenic cover with a high thread count. On top of that, place the deep-sided mattress pad with a pillowed top. Then the bottom sheet (also deep-sided or it will slip off), then your luxurious down duvet inside a hypoallergenic cover, which is then put inside the duvet cover of the same fabric as the bottom sheet and pillow cases. The duvet cover obviates the need for a top sheet, so there's no trapping of toes or twisted, tangled linens in the morning.

Now all you need are some chocolate chip cookies and a glass of cold milk.

Frozen Delights: Sorbet and a Little Ice Cream

Colder and wiser

Basic fruit sorbet

Chocolate tequila lime sorbet

Fig sorbet

Banana sorbet

Pear Champagne sorbet

Ginger ice cream

Ricotta ice cream

FROZEN DELIGHTS

Refreshing on a hot day and festive when it's cold outside, sorbet hits your palate with subdued flavors that heighten as it melts. A delicious way to extend the season for fragile fruit, juicy melons, ultra-ripe berries, peaches, kiwi or bananas; if it can be puréed or juiced, almost any fruit is fair game for sorbet.

Most recipes call for a simple syrup made by boiling sugar and water, then cooling the mixture and adding it to the fruit. If sugar will dissolve in the fruit, this step isn't necessary. After repeatedly testing both ways, we found no discernible difference in flavor or texture. In the Basic Fruit Sorbet recipe, simply combine all of the ingredients in a food processor or blender and then freeze.

If the fruit is firm, however, like apples or pears, or if there are brown sugar or other ingredients that require heat to dissolve properly, then a little cooking first is necessary. The Pear Champagne and the Banana Sorbet recipes are examples.

Sugar has a curious property in sorbet. Add too much and the sorbet won't freeze. If there's too little, the texture is grainy and icy. Sugar substitutes don't work at all. If your fruit is exceptionally sweet, add additional lemon or lime juice to balance the flavors. Once you've made a few batches, play with the addition of herbs and spices, or flavor with tea or wine, Champagne or cognac. The alcohol will inhibit freezing, so when experimenting, add ¼ cup or less to start. These recipes are only a starting point, enjoy the journey.

BASIC FRUIT SORBET

4 cups fruit purée
1 cup sugar
½ to 1 cup water or other non-alcoholic
    liquid
1 tablespoon lemon or lime juice, to taste

Note: *If the fruit is quite dense, like peaches, add all of the water. If there is a fair amount of liquid, as with watermelon, don't add any water.*

Blend all of the ingredients until smooth. If the fruit is objectionably seedy, strain it. Then freeze in an ice cream machine according to the manufacturer's instructions.

RANT ON ICE CREAM MACHINES

You do need an ice cream maker. Without one you'd end up with a big block of solidly frozen fruit ice. The machine whips air into the mixture as it freezes. Over the years we've owned all sorts of fancy and expensive ice cream making machines, all of which have broken and had to be shipped somewhere out of state to the only place in the USA where authorized repair could occur. The last time this happened, to hold me over until the machine was returned, I bought a $59 Krups ice cream maker and an extra freezer bowl and have never looked back. It works well, took years to wear out with constant usage, and when it did, I replaced it for the postage cost of returning the previous versions.

CHOCOLATE TEQUILA LIME SORBET

This frozen, dense chocolate sorbet added to the creamy Margarita Tapioca (page 47) with the same lime-tequila flavors makes your tastebuds think the accompanying garden-fresh fruit is even brighter and sweeter.

Makes 3 cups

½ pound bittersweet chocolate chipped into small pieces (Scharffen-Berger Bittersweet 70% is a good choice)
½ cup cocoa powder
¼ teaspoon salt
1½ cups water
½ cup tequila
2 teaspoons lime juice
⅔ cup plus 3 tablespoons sugar

Break up the chocolate into small pieces so that it will melt more easily. Place it in a bowl with the cocoa powder and salt. Put the water, tequila and sugar in a saucepan and bring to a boil to melt the sugar and cook off a little of the alcohol in the tequila. Pour the boiling mixture over the chocolate and stir to melt the chocolate completely. Cool the mixture and then add the lime juice. Freeze in an ice cream machine according to the manufacturer's directions.

FIG SORBET

1 quart very ripe fresh figs
1 cup sugar
½ cup Pinot Noir
½ cup water
1 tablespoon lemon juice
½ teaspoon freshly grated nutmeg

Remove the tough stem ends from the figs, chop them roughly and add them to a food processor along with the other ingredients. Purée untll smooth. Freeze in an ice cream machine according to the manufacturer's instructions.

BANANA SORBET

2 cups water
1 cup brown sugar
3 pounds unpeeled, very ripe bananas
2 tablespoons lime juice

Bring the water and sugar to a boil until the sugar has dissolved and the syrup has reduced a bit. Set it aside to cool. When the syrup is cool, peel the bananas and purée them in a mixer or food processor. Add the syrup and lime juice to the fruit and blend until you have a smooth mixture. If there are a few small pieces of banana, don't worry about it. Freeze according to your ice cream maker's directions. If you don't have an ice cream maker, place the mixture in a shallow pan and place in the freezer. After several hours, take a fork or use your mixer to blend the mixture until smooth. Let it freeze overnight.

PEAR CHAMPAGNE SORBET

Makes 1 quart

5 pears, peeled, cored and cut into cubes

1 cup Champagne or sparkling wine
    (Domaine Carneros, Schramsberg,
    Mumm Napa, Domaine Chandon,
    Frank Family...)

2 tablespoons Poire William or other pear-
    flavored liqueur (optional)

¾ cup sugar

½ teaspoon freshly grated nutmeg

1 teaspoon lemon juice

Simmer all ingredients in a medium saucepan over medium heat until the pears are soft and the alcohol has evaporated (10–15 minutes). Blend until smooth in a food processor. Chill the mixture in the refrigerator and then freeze in an ice cream machine according to the manufacturer's instructions.

GINGER ICE CREAM

2 cups whole milk

1 cup heavy cream

1 cup granulated sugar

3 tablespoons chopped peeled fresh
    ginger (from a 4-inch piece)

7 large egg yolks

Bring milk, cream, and ½ cup sugar to a boil in a 3-quart heavy saucepan. Remove the pan from the heat and stir in the ginger. Cover the pan and let the mixture steep for 25 minutes.

Whisk together the yolks and remaining ½ cup sugar in a mixing bowl. Add the ginger/milk mixture to the yolk mixture in a slow stream, whisking together. Transfer the mixture back to the saucepan. Cook over low heat, stirring constantly with a wooden spoon, until it's become a custard thick enough to coat the back of a spoon. Don't let it boil or you'll have scrambled eggs.

Pour the custard through a fine-mesh sieve into a metal bowl, discarding any solids, and cover with wax paper. Chill until cold, about 1½ hours. Freeze in an ice cream maker according to the manufacturer's instructions, and then put the ice cream in an airtight container in the freezer to harden for at least 4 hours.

RICOTTA ICE CREAM

The first time I had fresh ricotta cheese, it was a revelation. Michael Coon, formerly of the Culinary Institute and now somewhere in the wilds of Mexico, introduced me to Cindy Callahan of Bellwether Farms in Petaluma. She and her son, Liam, against all odds, were making sheep's milk cheese in a country where sheep are raised for lamb chops, not milking. With persistence and passion they were breeding more voluptuous gals, and making outstanding cheeses in the bargain. Their ricotta is available occasionally at Dean & DeLuca and I'm not above begging when one of the Callahans visits a local Farmers' Market. With the growth of wonderful fresh cheeses all over the country, it's worth contacting your favorite cheese purveyor or cheese maker in your area to see if they have fresh ricotta available.

Serves 12

2½ cups milk

1½ cups sugar

4 large egg yolks

3⅓ cups fresh ricotta, sheep's milk if available

1 cup heavy cream, well chilled

2 tablespoons dark rum

Combine the milk and half the sugar in a medium saucepan and bring to a boil. Meanwhile, in a heat-proof bowl, combine the egg yolks with the remaining sugar and beat, preferably with an electric mixer, until the mixture is pale and thick enough to hold its shape when a ribbon of it is trailed across the surface. Pour in some of the hot milk in a thin stream, whisking steadily, until the yolks are warmed. Then whisk the yolk mixture into the remaining hot milk in the saucepan. Put it on a flame tamer so that the pan is not in direct contact with the heat (or place a cast-iron frying pan upside down over, but not touching, the flame and put your pot on top of that).

Use a wooden spoon to stir the custard frequently. It will take 20 minutes or so to reach 185° and thicken. Continue to cook the custard until it coats the back of the spoon and holds a clear line when you drag a finger through it. Remove the pan from the heat and plunge the base in cold water.

Add ricotta and mix vigorously until thoroughly combined. Remove the bowl from the cold water bath, cover it and refrigerate until the custard is chilled.

Stir the cream and rum into the chilled ricotta custard. Pour the mixture into the ice cream machine and churn, following the manufacturer's instructions, until the mix has frozen to a consistency firm enough to serve or store.

Pantry

Ingredients for the palate

Red chile purée

Aioli

Harissa

Goreme

Jalapeño mustard

Romesco sauce

Oak Knoll Inn 5-chile ketchup

Pesto sauce

Drunken jalapeños

Blue cheese crackers

Lemon curd

Dilly beans

Onion crackers

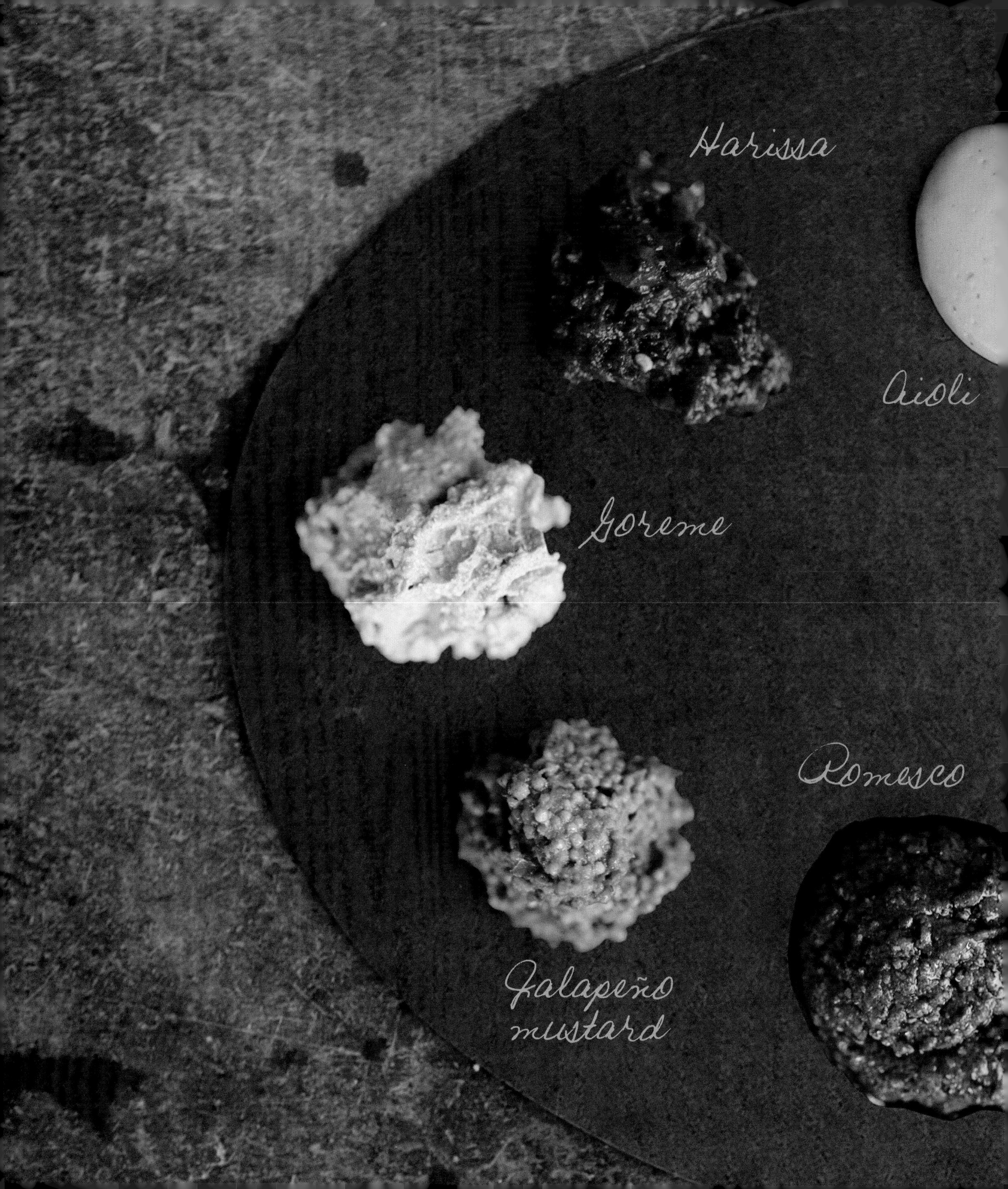

Harissa

Aioli

Goreme

Romesco

Jalapeño
mustard

Red chile
sauce

White bean
spread

Red chile
purée

RED CHILE PURÉE

Our garden is prolific with chiles each summer, so we dry some and prepare this chile purée for the layered tortilla omelet on page 39 where it adds great depth of flavor to the red chile sauce. It freezes well, is a welcome addition to soups and stews, and can be used when making quesadillas. If you don't have a garden or a Mexican/Latin American market in your neighborhood, many supermarkets carry dried chiles in a Mexican section.

6 ounces of dried chiles: pasilla, New Mexico, California, and/or negra

A word of warning, don't wear white when making this.

Remove the stem and seeds from the dry chiles and then toast them over high heat in a dry skillet or comal. This will only take a couple of minutes. The chile will change color and there will be a bit of smoke when they're ready. If you go too far, the resulting purée will be quite bitter, so don't blacken the chiles.

When they're toasted, place the chiles in a saucepan and cover them with water. Bring to a boil, cover and then simmer for 10 minutes. Remove the pan from the heat and let everything cool for a few minutes. Drain the chiles but reserve the water.

Purée the chiles in a blender or food processor with as much of the reserved water as necessary to make a fairly loose purée, similar to the consistency of ketchup. Strain the purée through a medium sieve to remove any stray seeds and skin.

WHITE BEAN SPREAD

1 pound fresh shelled white beans or ½ pound dried beans, soaked overnight
1 leek, washed and trimmed of dark green parts
1 carrot, scraped clean
1 onion, medium-size, peeled
1 clove
2 teaspoons salt

In a large saucepan, put the beans, leek, carrot, peeled onion with the clove stuck in it. Cover with cool water and bring the mixture to a boil over high heat. Skim off any gunk that floats to the top.

Add salt, reduce heat to low, cover and simmer for half an hour or so until the beans are tender. (You'll need closer to 2 hours if the beans were dried.) Drain in a colander and discard everything but the beans.

2 garlic cloves, peeled and crushed
¼ cup mustard – use Dijon or Jalapeño
½ cup Champagne vinegar
1 cup extra virgin olive oil
Salt and freshly ground pepper
30 mint leaves, finely chopped

Pulse the beans, parsley and garlic in a food processor or use a mixing bowl and mash with a fork. Whisk in the mustard, vinegar and salt. Pour the olive oil into the mixture in a steady stream, whisking constantly until you get the consistency of mayonnaise.

Grind a generous amount of fresh pepper over the top and garnish with chopped mint. Serve with toasted baguette slices or pita.

AIOLI

Our aioli – with one whole egg rather than lots of yolks as is traditional in Provence – is a relatively low-cholesterol version. The eggs, when we're fortunate, come from Long Meadow Ranch here in Napa. From organically raised, lovingly treated and cherished chickens, the eggs have luscious yellow-orange yolks and look like Easter eggs – blue, green, creamy tan and a deep rich brown. If you live in an area where you're not confident in your producer, buy pasteurized eggs at the market.

Makes 1 cup

1 whole egg
4 large cloves fresh garlic, crushed
1 teaspoon dry mustard
½ teaspoon salt
½ teaspoon freshly ground white pepper
¼ to ½ teaspoon cayenne (depending
    on how spicy you like your food)
Juice from ½ a lemon (2–3 tablespoons)
1 cup subtly flavored California olive oil

Traditionally, aioli is served in the south of France with crudités. In addition to raw vegetables, we like it with grilled fish or chicken, or use it as a salad dressing or replacement for mayonnaise on sandwiches, in potato salad, and in the jicama slaw on page 31.

Place all ingredients except olive oil in a blender (or use an immersion blender). Cover and blend at medium speed until thoroughly combined. Remove the cover, and with the blender running, very slowly pour the olive oil in a stream into the mixture until it emulsifies and thickens. Chill and let the flavors combine for at least an hour.

HARISSA

A fixture on Moroccan tables, harissa is a spicy red pepper condiment. As we grow a variety of peppers each year, the garden and how the peppers taste tend to determine the proportion of different types of peppers. I use some sweet red bell peppers for a solid pepper background taste, and then build on that with hotter varieties.

2 red bell peppers, roasted and peeled

10–12 hot red chiles – jalapeños, habañeros, cayenne, arboles, serranos… whatever's fresh, wonderful and available

2 cloves garlic, peeled

2 teaspoons caraway seeds

½ teaspoon coriander seeds

½ teaspoon cumin seed

Salt – probably a teaspoon but if you're salt-phobic, use ½

¼ to ½ cup olive oil

Roast and peel the bell peppers.

Don't peel the hot peppers. Get rid of the hard stem bits and roughly chop the rest, including the seeds.

Put the caraway, coriander and cumin seeds in a small dry skillet, turn on the gas to medium-high, and when you start to smell the spices, shake the pan as though you're making popcorn the old-fashioned way. When they start to smell again, set the pan aside to cool.

Put everything except the olive oil in a food processor (or mortar and pestle or blender if you don't have a processor) and let 'er rip. Add enough olive oil – slowly – to make the harissa about the texture of a thick spaghetti sauce. Put it in a jar, smooth the top and pour a film of olive oil over it. Refrigerate until you use it up.

Hint: *For your guests who reach for water to put out the heat – milk or cheese or a piece of bread work much better. Water just spreads it around.*

Roasting and peeling peppers: Place each pepper over an open gas flame on your stove if you have gas, or under the broiler, or on a grill. Char the skin – get it blackened – then run the pepper under cold water, peeling off the skin as you go. Pull or cut out the stem, seeds and membrane. Some recipes will tell you to put the blackened peppers in a bowl and cover with plastic wrap, or in a plastic bag. This steams them so the skins loosen and come off, but it also changes the flavor and texture of the peppers. For this recipe, fresher and sweeter red peppers combine with the hot peppers to give a complex layered flavor.

GOREME
Hot Spicy Cheese

This is a variation of a Turkish recipe from one of my favorite cookbooks and cookbook authors, *Tapas to Meze* by Joanne Weir. We had our usual motherlode of hot peppers in the garden and were looking for different ways to use them. Layers of flavor come from the three different fresh spicy peppers, but you can substitute a teaspoon of cayenne to get back to Joanne's delicious original recipe.

1¼ cups yogurt (if you can find it, use Skyhill goat cheese yogurt)

10 ounces feta cheese

2 crushed garlic cloves

1 fresh cayenne pepper, minced

1 red jalapeño pepper, minced

1 serrano pepper, minced

1 teaspoon ground paprika

1 tablespoon extra virgin olive oil

Salt and freshly ground pepper to taste

TO MAKE THE YOGURT CHEESE

Place a strainer over a bowl and line it with cheesecloth or use a coffee filter. Put the yogurt in the strainer and let all of the liquid whey drain off overnight in the refrigerator. Discard the whey.

TO MIX THE GOREME

Place the yogurt and feta cheeses in a bowl. Add everything but the salt and pepper and blend with a fork or pulse in a food processor or blender until it's almost smooth, but still a little chunky. Add salt and freshly ground pepper to taste. If the feta is particularly salty, you might not want to add any additional salt. Serve with bread or pita.

JALAPEÑO MUSTARD

Served at the 4th of July picnic, this mustard is great by itself served with a baguette, can be used as a condiment and spread on sandwiches, or mixed with Napa Valley olive oil to make a marinade for poultry, beef, lamb or pork using a ratio of 2 parts mustard to 3 parts oil. We grow the jalapeños in our garden, along with other spicy peppers, so occasionally we'll substitute a habañero or two, a red bonnet, or one of the Thai chiles for one of the jalapeños. Adjust to the asbestos qualities of your palate.

Makes 1 cup

½ cup mustard powder
½ cup whole mustard seeds
1 tablespoon cumin seeds, toasted lightly
    in a sauté pan until they release their
    flavor and then crushed in a mortar
    and pestle
3 jalapeño peppers, seeds and
    membrane removed
2 cloves garlic
1 teaspoon salt
⅓ cup red wine vinegar
¼ cup water
¼ cup brown sugar

Purée all ingredients in a blender until mixed thoroughly. Keep tightly covered in a jar and refrigerate for 2 weeks to a month before using.

ROMESCO SAUCE

Every Catalan cook in Spain has her (his) own recipe for romesco. It's used with grilled meats, cheeses, vegetables, breads, and as a side dish. This recipe is a variation on one I learned from Ann Walker when she introduced a number of Spanish dishes to a group of us at Gloria Ferrar winery.

Makes 5 cups (can be refrigerated for a couple of weeks)

1 cup almonds

3 1-inch-thick slices sour dough bread

6 garlic cloves, unpeeled

2 red bell peppers, stemmed, seeded and roughly chopped

6 tomatoes, quartered

2 cloves garlic, peeled

3 tablespoons paprika

1 teaspoon salt

1 teaspoon freshly ground black pepper

1 tablespoon hot red pepper flakes – we use a mixture of dried habañero, serrano, jalapeño and others from the garden

2 cups olive oil

1 cup red wine vinegar

Preheat oven to 400°. Place the almonds, bread and unpeeled garlic on a baking sheet in the oven for about 15 minutes until you start to smell the nuts roasting. Break-up the bread and place it with the almonds in a food processor until finely ground.

Peel and add the baked garlic, along with the peppers, tomatoes, fresh garlic, paprika, salt, black pepper and pepper flakes. Process until smooth. With the motor running, gradually add the oil and then the vinegar until the sauce is thick, smooth and emulsified.

OAK KNOLL INN 5-CHILE KETCHUP

In September the Tyranny of the Tomatoes starts in the garden and we're overwhelmed with produce. That's the signal to pull out the huge kettle and make as much of this ketchup as we can fit into the pan. It makes the kitchen smell wonderful and lasts until next season in the freezer. In addition to the traditional use on burgers and fries, spread a little on a quesadilla or grilled cheese sandwich before cooking so it melts into the cheese.

Makes 7–8 cups

4 each roasted and minced jalapeño, cayenne, and Fresno chiles (or any others that are wonderful in the garden; if using habañeros, use caution with the number that you add and use rubber gloves when handling, especially if you wear contacts)

6 cups roasted, peeled and puréed fresh tomatoes – use romas or other pulpy variety

1 large white or yellow onion, chopped

1 small red onion, chopped

2 tablespoons olive oil

3 cloves garlic, minced

1 cup sugar – use less if the tomatoes are particularly sweet

2 tablespoons toasted and ground cumin seed

2 tablespoons toasted and ground oregano

1 teaspoon cinnamon

1 teaspoon freshly grated nutmeg

2 cups rice vinegar

8 cloves garlic, roasted and crushed

2 tablespoons dried and crushed New Mexico red chiles

1 tablespoon dried and crushed ancho chile

1 cup sun-dried tomatoes (we dry our own Sweet-100s and use those for the sweetness)

1 large bunch of cilantro, stems and leaves chopped

Salt to taste

Freshly ground pepper

To roast the tomatoes and peppers, put them in large roasting pan, dribble a little olive oil over them and place in a 450° oven. Reduce the heat to 350° and roast for 45 minutes to an hour until they smell wonderful and have a little char on them. At that point the skins will slide off the tomatoes very easily. Remove the skins and as much of the watery liquid and seeds as you can, but you don't need to be fanatical about it.

In a 6-quart saucepan or dutch oven, sauté the onions lightly in olive oil until soft. Add minced garlic and sauté a little longer. Add sugar and cook until it forms a glaze – 5–7 minutes.

Add the cumin, oregano, cinnamon and nutmeg and deglaze with the vinegar to get up all of the little cooked bits. Keep the mixture bubbling for 10 minutes or so to reduce the vinegar while you assemble the remaining ingredients.

Add the chiles, tomatoes and cilantro.

Simmer over low heat for 2–3 hours. Allow to cool and then purée. Add salt and freshly ground pepper to taste. Refrigerate. You can serve it right away, but it's even better after a day or so, and keeps for weeks in the refrigerator and freezes well.

Cumin seeds

To toast cumin seeds, place them in a hot skillet and shake it until you notice their aroma. Add the oregano and toss them together for another minute. Then grind them with a mortar and pestle or a coffee grinder you use only for spices.

PESTO SAUCE

This classic Italian basil sauce is traditionally made with pine nuts. Here we've used almonds, and I've also substituted hazelnuts and even macadamias when the mood, menu and supply dictated. In Liguria, the traditional version calls for fresh oregano and walnuts. For a latin approach, substitute cilantro. In addition to the omelet on page 197, pesto can be tossed with pasta or steamed spring potatoes, added to tomato sauce or vegetable soup, or mixed with buttermilk and sour cream to create a salad dressing. It can also be frozen in small batches for use sometime in winter when you want a burst of summer on your palate.

Makes ¾ cup

2 cups fresh basil, stems removed
4 garlic cloves, peeled
½ cup blanched almonds, coarsely
    chopped
⅓ cup extra-virgin olive oil, divided
½ cup grated Parmesan
½ teaspoon salt
Freshly ground black pepper, to taste

Place the basil, garlic and nuts in a food processor and process until everything is chopped to an even consistency. Add half the olive oil in a slow steady stream with the machine running. Turn off the processor and add the cheese. Process again until the cheese is well incorporated and then slowly add the remaining oil with the machine running. Taste for salt and pepper.

If you're not going to use it immediately, put the pesto in a container, cover it with a thin layer of oil and store it in the refrigerator as it will loose its color quickly.

DRUNKEN JALAPEÑOS

Choose jalapeños that are perfect, with blemish-free, firm, smooth skins. We grow our own and let them ripen to the red stage, which gives them an additional sweetness and flavor, but green ones are fine. Save the marinating liquid and blend it with some extra-virgin olive oil for a wonderful salad dressing or marinade for grilled vegetables.

2½ to 3 pounds fresh jalapeño
    peppers, grilled slightly
A fifth of tequila
2 cups cider vinegar
2 cinnamon sticks
10 whole cloves
10 whole allspice
Salt to taste

Lightly grill whole jalapeño peppers so they develop a bit of blackened char on the skin. Bring the rest of the ingredients to a boil in a non-aluminum saucepan. Put the peppers in a sterilized jar and pour the pickling ingredients over them. Let the peppers marinate in the jar in the refrigerator for a week or so, and then enjoy!

BLUE CHEESE CRACKERS

Shirlee often makes these to serve with Bell Winery Cabernet or Vincent Arroyo's Port, when we're lucky enough to get some of it. They also pair well with the melon and prosciutto on page 84.

Makes about 30

8 ounces Gorgonzola or other blue cheese, crumbled

1 stick butter (4 ounces) at room temperature

1 cup all-purpose flour

½ teaspoon salt

Place butter and cheese in a bowl and blend them with a fork until creamy. Add flour and salt and mix until all of the ingredients are incorporated. Form dough into a cylinder the size you would like your crackers to be – about the size of a silver dollar – and wrap in waxed paper or plastic wrap. Refrigerate until firm (3 hours or overnight). Slice dough into rounds ⅛-inch thick and place on a cold, greased baking sheet 2 inches apart. Bake until golden brown, about 12 minutes in a preheated 375° oven.

LEMON CURD

Makes 1½ cups

3 egg yolks

Grated zest of 2 lemons

Juice from 2 lemons (approximately ¼ cup)

½ cup sugar

¼ cup unsalted butter, cut into 10 or more pieces so it melts quickly

Place the yolks and sugar in the top of a double boiler set over simmering water. Beat them until the mixture thickens and it turns pale yellow. Beat in the zest and juice. Stir in the butter until it melts. Continue to cook, stirring frequently, for about 15 minutes until the mixture is thick and becomes the consistency of mayonnaise. (Don't let it come to a boil or you'll have lemon scrambled eggs.)

Seal remainder in sterilized jars. Lemon curd will keep for several months in the refrigerator. In addition to the chocolate toast pillows (page 117), it can be used as a filling for layer cakes or served in a pre-baked tart shell.

DILLY BEANS

This is a variation of an old Vermont recipe for pickled green beans, canned in the summer to be served with cinnamon doughnuts and sugar-on-snow at maple syrup time. As we produce neither maple syrup nor snow here in Napa, but do have green beans in the garden and market most of the year, I make them fresh. The texture is firmer than the canned version, the salt doesn't get absorbed and the flavor is brighter with a nice little zing from the garlic and cayenne. They will keep in the refrigerator for several weeks.

Makes 1 quart

2 to 3 heads of just-picked dill

1 quart fresh, firm, perfect string beans

2 tablespoons salt

¼ teaspoon cayenne pepper

2 large cloves garlic, sliced

1 cup white vinegar

2 to 3 cups cold water

Place the dill in a non-aluminum saucepan (vinegar and aluminum bring out the worst in each other). Trim the stem ends off the string beans and put them on top of the dill. Sprinkle with the salt, cayenne and garlic. Pour vinegar over the top, then the water. The beans should be just covered with liquid. If not, add more water. Bring to a boil quickly over high heat, then simmer on low until the beans lose their bright green color – approximately 4 minutes. Remove from the heat and allow the beans to cool in the brine for at least 2 hours, and then chill in the refrigerator before serving.

ONION CRACKERS

These crackers are crispy and savory and add a welcome crunch and piquancy alongside a creamy egg dish on those mornings when you don't feel like baking muffins or bread. They're also a popular feature at our evening wine-tasting party where they pair well with cheese.

2 cups all-purpose flour

1 teaspoon baking powder

1 tablespoon sugar

2 teaspoons salt

¼ teaspoon freshly ground pepper

1 egg at room temperature

⅓ cup vegetable oil

1 cup finely chopped onion

2 tablespoons water (or more if needed)

TO MAKE THE DOUGH

Combine the dry ingredients – flour, baking powder, sugar and salt and pepper – in a large mixing bowl.

Combine the remaining ingredients in another bowl and then slowly pour them into the dry ingredients, mixing with a wooden spoon (or food processor or electric mixer) to form a firm dough. Add water as necessary to make the dough come together. Knead it briefly, or as long as it takes to become smooth. Place the dough in a buttered bowl. Cover the bowl with a plate or use plastic wrap and place it in the refrigerator for 30 minutes or more.

TO BAKE

Preheat oven to 375°.

Remove the chilled and rested dough from the refrigerator and divide it into 2 parts. Cover one part as you work with the other. Press and roll the dough into a rectangle about the length of your baking sheet. Roll the dough as thinly as possible without tearing it, about ⅛-inch thick.

Transfer the dough to a lightly greased baking sheet, using the rolling pin to help you move it. With a pizza cutter or knife, cut it into 2 x 2-inch crackers. Repeat with the remaining dough. Bake the ends and odd pieces as well. They're tasty and this is not a refined-looking cracker, so odd shapes are fine and provide something for kitchen helpers to taste. Using a fork, prick each cracker several times to help it stay flat during baking.

Bake at 375° for 10–15 minutes until lightly browned. The crackers can be eaten immediately or cooled and stored in an airtight container for up to a week.

4 eggs
1 cup so
3/4 cup Flo
1/4 cup cocoa
T.P. bak

2
1 c. berries

chac dp

5 T melted bu

yolks + sour cream
Add flw & b.s.
Stir in buttermilk 1 c
Add melted butter
mix thoroughly
beat egg whites

Resources

FOR THE BEST SPECIALITY INGREDIENTS AND EQUIPMENT USED

CHOCOLATE

ANNETTE'S CHOCOLATE

Chocolate disks, wine-chocolate sauces
1321 First Street
Napa, Ca 94559
707-252-4228
www.anettes.com

BISSINGER'S HANDCRAFTED CHOCOLATIER

Wine and chocolate tasting kit, solid chocolate, chocolate-covered raspberries and blackberries in season
3983 Gratiot Street
St. Louis, MO 63110
314-615-2424
www.bissingers.com

CHOCOHOLICS DIVINE DESSERTS

For chocolate pasta and other creative uses of the food of the gods
18819 East Hwy 88
Clements, CA 95227
1-800-760-CHOC (2462)
www.gourmetchocolate.com

SCHARFFEN BERGER CHOCOLATE MAKER

Bars, cocoa powder, nibs, artisan producers of quality chocolate
Factory: 914 Heinz Avenue, Berkeley, CA 94710
800-930-4528
www.scharffenberger.com

LINENS AND TABLETOP

FRETTE

For beautiful sheets and linens
1-800-353-7388
1-212-299-0474
www.frette.com

VANDERBILT

Linens, tabletop, gifts
1429 Main Street
St. Helena, CA 94574
707-963-1010

OLIVE OIL

COOC certified (California Olive Oil Council)

www.oliveoilsource.com

LILA JAEGER OLIVE OIL

Our neighbor to the north, Lila was one of the pioneers in the resurgence of the California olive oil industry
5100 Big Ranch Road
Napa, CA 94558
707-257-2227
email: jaegerevo@gmail.com

THE OLIVE PRESS

Producers and purveyors of a variety of oils, vinegars, related serving pieces and linens
The Oxbow Public Market, First Street, Napa, CA 94558
and Jacuzzi Winery
24724 Arnold Drive
Highway 121
Sonoma, CA 95476
www.theolivepress.com

McEVOY OLIVE OIL

High quality olive oil from a beautiful property. Tours by appointment
5935 Red Hill Road
Petaluma, CA 94952
866-617-6779 or 707-778-2307
www.mcevoyranch.com

DaVERO SONOMA

Ridgeley Evers was a creator of the modern California olive and olive oil industry. (I hesitate to call it something so businesslike.) The source for olive oil, trees, wine, fun
1195 Westside Rod
Healdsburg, CA 95448
888-431-8008 or 707-431-8000
www.davero.com

LONG MEADOW RANCH

Organically and sustainably produced wine, olive oil, grass-fed beef, eggs, fruit and vegetables.
Long Meadow Ranch Garden Stand
1796 South St. Helena Highway
707-963-4555
www.longmeadowranch.com

HERBS AND SPICES

FORNI-BROWN

Vegetable and herb suppliers to local restaurants and the source of plants for our vegetable gardens. Everything they grow is grown for flavor. Vegetable starts and seeds available in the Spring.
Cedar and Pine Streets, Calistoga, CA
707-942-6123

WHOLE SPICE

Wonderful fresh spices and unique mixtures, including *ras-al-hanout* and a kefta blend for Moroccan menus
Shuli and Ronit Madmone, owners
Oxbow Public Market
610 First Street, #13
Napa, CA 94559
707-256-0700
www.wholespice.com

PENZEY'S SPICES

Spices, tools, chocolate supplies
800-741-7787
www.penzeys.com

CHEESE

JOHN RAYMOND CHEESEMONGER

Known to court a farmer for two years to get a wheel of cheese produced from milk of a cow only allowed to eat the top two inches of grass. He's THE source for the best.
RAYMOND & CO.
The Vats, Jack London Village
14301 Arnold Drive
Glen Ellen, CA 95442
707-938-9911
www.raymondcheesemongers.com

SOME OF OUR FAVORITE CALIFORNIA CHEESEMAKERS

BELLWETHER FARMS

Sheep and cow cheeses: Carmody, Crescenza, ricotta, San Andreas
888-527-8606
Sonoma County, CA
www.bellwetherfarms.com

BRAVO FARMS

Handmade Cheeses
Edam, Clothbound Cheddar, Gouda
36005 Hwy 99
Traver, CA 93673
559-897-4634
www.bravofarms.com

COWGIRL CREAMERY

Mt. Tam, Red Hawk, artisan cheeses, sustainably produced
80 Fourth Street, Point Reyes Station, CA 94956
415-663-9335
866-433-7834
www.cowgirlcreamery.com

CYPRESS GROVE CHEVRE

Humboldt Fog, goat milk cheddar, Purple Haze
1330 Q Street
Arcata, CA
707-825-1100
www.cypressgrovechevre.com

FISCALINI CHEESE COMPANY

San Joaquin Gold, 18-month cheddar
Founded in 1917
Modesto, California
1-800-610-FARM
www.fiscalinicheese.com

HARLEY FARMS GOAT DAIRY

Feta, fromage blanc, ricotta
205 North Street
P.O Box 173
Pescadero, CA 94060
800-879-0480
www.harleyfarms.com

MEYENBERG GOAT MILK PRODUCTS

Use in dulce de leche
free of hormones, antibiotics and preservatives
www.meyenberg.com

ROUGE ET NOIR

Specializing in soft ripening cheeses
Marin French Cheese Co. 7500 Red Hill Road
Petaluma, CA 94952
800-292-6001 x112
www.marinfrenchcheese.com

SIERRA NEVADA CHEESE COMPANY

Delicious cow and goat's milk cheeses, cream cheese, butter, from hormone-free and antibiotic-free critters.
6505 County Road 39
Willows, CA 95988
www.sierranevadacheese.com

SKYHILL NAPA VALLEY FARMS

Goat cheeses, yogurt, from happy Napa goats
P.O. Box 5029, Napa, CA 94581
707-255-4800
888-512-4628
www.skyhillfarms.com

STRAUS FAMILY CREAMERY

Organic dairy products: milk, cheese, butter, and yogurt
Marshall, CA
www.strausfamilycreamery.com

VELLA CHEESE

Jack, aged jack, Italian, cheddar…
Ig Vella, owner
315 Second Street East
Sonoma, CA 95476
www.vellacheese.com

KITCHEN TOOLS AND SUPPLIES

NAPA STYLE

Chef Michael Chiarello's cooking implements, tabletop accessories, wine country furnishings and every wine-related tool imaginable
866-776-1600
V Marketplace
6525 Washington St., Yountville, CA
www.napastyle.com

SHACKFORD'S KITCHEN STORE

In addition to a huge variety of kitchen tools and supplies, Mr. Shackford also stocks parts. If you need an extra bowl for your ice cream machine, a new paddle for your mixer, a new top for a pan – he's the guy to call. Everyone in the shop is helpful and very nice.
1350 Main Street
Napa, CA 94559
707-226-2132

DEAN & DELUCA

Purveyors of kitchenware, serving pieces, chocolate, caviar, wine, cheese…
800-221-7714
www.deandeluca.com

WILLIAMS SONOMA

Kitchenware, table linens, chocolate
877-812-6235
www.williams-sonoma.com

SUR LA TABLE

Kitchen equipment, tableware and linens, serving pieces, cooking classes
800-243-0852
www.surlatable.com

INDESPENSIBLE AND WITHOUT CATEGORY

KATI KOOS

Interesting serving pieces, unique tabletop accessories, party clothes and a huge number of things that don't fit into any category
500 Sutter Street
San Francisco, CA 94102
415-362-3437
www.katikoos.com

MOROCCO TOUR-GUIDE PAR EXCELLENCE

CHAAL HOUSSEIN
Chaal is extremely knowledgeable about Morocco and helped me track down recipes, special tajines and ceramic serving pieces for the Inn, fabrics and rugs, artists and architectural pieces. He's hosted groups from Stanford, the Smithsonian, archeologists and researchers of all types. He's a joy to be with and a delightful gentleman.
Cell phone in Morocco is: 00 212 61 160730
email: chaal_houssein@usa.net

BRUCE AIDELLS SAUSAGES

Chicken apple, mango and habañero…
Available at meat markets and through the internet.
www.aidells.com

HOG ISLAND OYSTER COMPANY

Founded in 1983 by three marine biologists to produce local, high-quality, sustainably raised oysters
20215 Highway 1
Marshall, CA 94940
415-663-9218
www.hogislandoysters.com

TSAR NICOLAI CAVIAR

Pioneers of sustainable California caviar
60 Dorman Avenue
San Francisco, CA 94124
1-800-95-CAVIAR
www.tsarnicoulai.com

INDEX

Page numbers in **bold** type indicate photographs